Fletcher Chambliss Jr

HOW TO SAY "NO" TO SIN GOD'S WAY

How to Say NO to Sin God's Way

HOW TO SAY "NO" TO SIN GOD'S WAY

THE BOOK OF ROMANS

CHAPTER'S 5,6,7,8

FLETCHER CHAMBLISS JR

If you really believe that **Romans 8:31** is true, then you will live your life like **Hebrews 13:5-6**, because you will be Fully Convinced (**Romans 4:20-25**), that with **God All things are Possible (Matthew 19:26, Mark 10:27, Luke 18:27)**.
Fletcher Chambliss Jr.
Romans 11:36
www.llaac.com

The Holy Bible, New International Version, NIV
Copyright ©1973, 1978, 1984, 2011 by Biblica, Inc. Used by permission
Certain Stock Imagery © Thinkstock

Printed in the United States of America
ISBN: 978-1-7331540-0-0 (softcover)
ISBN: 978-1-7331540-3-1 (e-book)

Library of Congress Control# 2018930087

Non-Fiction/ self-Help/ Christian Living

.

FCJLLC
2331 Deer Pass Way
Decatur GA 30035
www.llaac.com

CONTENTS

PREFACE

I dedicate this book to all Born Again Christians who are struggling with sin and temptation in their lives. I hope this book will teach them how they can have victory over their sins and temptations and show them that God has had a plan from the very beginning that would allow all Born Again Believers to have victory over their sins through Him because we can do nothing in this world without Him. Everything that happens to a believer during their lifetime must be allowed by God and be a part of His planned purpose for that person's life. I thank God the Father, my Lord and Savior Jesus Christ and The Holy Spirit for allowing me to write this book for them under Their guidance and protection. God protected me from the demons that satan had sent after me to prevent me from writing this book. I witnessed this warfare inside of my house one morning after I had finished writing for that night (I had stayed up all night writing until 6:00 am the next morning). You know how sometimes you see something move from the corner of your eye, and then when you look in that direction there is nothing there? This happens to most of us all the time, so we just blow it off as nothing important, but this morning I saw something move from the corner of my eye and when I looked in that direction, as usual, there was nothing there, but then I saw something move from the corner of my other eye and then my other eye until these movements begin to appear all around my living room from one side to the other until I could see them clearly, and then I knew that I was not alone anymore. As I watched these movements, I then realized that something was trying to get to me, but something or someone was preventing these demons from reaching me, and when I saw that they could not get to me, I then realized that God had sent some Angels to protect me from harm. So, I sat there and watched all of this activity for a few minutes, watching what looked like shimmers moving from one side of my living room to the other, (I was scared at first), but when I realized that I was being protected by God I then relaxed and laid down on my sofa and fell fast to sleep. What I saw is kind of hard to explain because I saw no shapes just shimmers in the air. Have you ever looked outside on a very hot day and you could see waves of heat moving through the air, (I call them shimmers), and that's what I saw moving from one side of my living room to the other? I would see 3 shimmering lines, and then they would disappear and then re-appear on the other side of the room, and then they would disappear again and re-appear somewhere else in the room as if someone was chasing them or fighting with them.   God allowed me to witness this with my own eyes to prove to me that nothing can happen to me without His approval, because He is in control of everything and everyone, and nothing happens in this world without His permission.   I want to say Thank You to God my Father, Jesus Christ my Lord and Savior and The Holy Spirit for my salvation and for protecting me from satan and his demons.   And last but not least I want to thank my family and friends for putting up with me as I have lived my life and for being there for me when I needed them.   I hope this book will help all Christians everywhere and teach them how they can have victory over the sin and temptation in their life, which should bring them more peace and joy to their everyday life.   Always remember to go to God for whatever you need in your life, He loves us and will take care of us His way.   Take care, God loves you all, and so do I Amen.

CHAPTER ONE

My People are Destroyed for The Lack of Knowledge!!!

The message you are about to read is what God is teaching me concerning sin and temptation in my life and how I can have victory over them. All of the information you are about to read is working for me and has changed me into the man I am today. A man that is not afraid to face his sins and temptations anymore because God is teaching me that I can control them with His help and that He will be with me every step of the way helping me with this sin battle until the day I die. By the time you finish this book, you should have a different outlook on God and the sin that is in your life, because you will understand for yourself the Love and Power of God in the scripture teachings of this message. The scriptures this book will tell you to read and study should draw you closer to God and Christ and help you have victory over the sin in your life. No one should have to tell you anymore that God is real, it is one thing when you hear other people talk about God but when you finally experience God for yourself, (feel His presence and hear His quiet voice), from that moment until the day that you die, no one will be able to tell you that God is not real or that He does not exist, because you will know without a shadow of doubt for yourself that He is real. As you read this book you will be tempted by sin, you will sin, and you will learn how God has set us free from sin and temptation so that we can live for Him as we should and complete His planned purpose for our lives. If you believe in God and what He has written in His Holy Word the Bible, then victory over sin is the gift that He offers to everyone who believes in Him. You must be a Christian for this message to help you, a Born Again Christian. If you are not a Born Again Christian, then you are not a Christian at all, and if you died right now you would go to **Hell.** If you want to become a Christian there is a Prayer for Salvation in the back of this book, please pray this Prayer to God and ask Him to come into your life and save you, and then you will become a Born Again Christian.

Have you ever wondered why most pastors do not teach on the subject of how to have victory over Sin, and as a matter of fact, most Christians you know never talk about the subject either?   There can be only one reason for this because they are not having Victory over sin themselves.   Learning how to say no to sin and temptation is probably the most important teaching that all Christians will need to hear, and then receive proper instruction teaching them how to live it out in their everyday Christian life.   Knowing how to live for God by having victory over the sin in their life is something every believer will use and practice every day in their Christian life.   Without this information they will be defeated by satan over and over again in their daily Christian life as I was, and just as most Born Again Christians are today.   Satan is going to try to tempt us to sin every day of our Christian life, (until the day we die), so we must get ready for the battle, by learning what to do when he attacks.

I have heard many good pastors preach on all sorts of topics, but of those same preachers, I have not heard any of them preach on how to have victory over sin.   I have heard some that began to preach on the subject of having victory over sin, but they never tell you how to do it, nor give a good detailed teaching on how to say no to sin.   In most churches the only teaching you get on how to deal with sin is to;

1. Look up and memorize scriptures relating to your sin so you can use them against satan when he tempts you, or
2. Fast and pray.

Now there is nothing wrong with fasting and praying and memorizing scriptures, these are good Christian practices to learn.   But remember that satan attacked Jesus after He fasted and used Bible scriptures during some of his attacks, so he knows the Bible better than most Christians **(Matthew 4:2-11 and Luke 4:3-12)**.   Memorizing the Bible to defeat satan will not work if you do not believe what you are reading, and fasting is an outside measure used by men/women to get God's attention, they fast to let Him know that they agree with Him concerning the sin in their life.   Because the majority of Born Again Christians are being defeated by sin daily, proves that we do not believe what we read in the Bible.   The Bible teaches believers everything that they will need to know about having victory over sin and temptation, all they need to do is to read it, and then practice what the Bible teaches. The two disciplines above should be practiced by every Christian, (memorizing scriptures and fasting and prayer), but they will not give you victory over sin and temptation.   I know because I have tried them both, and I am here to tell you that none of them worked for me, I still continued to sin when I was tempted.   You can memorize the whole Bible if you choose to or go on all of the 30 day fasts that your body can endure, this still will not stop you from sinning, because sin is inside of you, sin is in your flesh apart of your D.N.A. (**Romans 5:12 and 7:17-23**).   Sin must be dealt with from the inside, not the outside.   You cannot use outside measures to fix an inside problem.   And the only person that can change us from the inside is God, through salvation, coming from the Cross of Jesus Christ, being Born Again and filled with the Holy Spirit of God.   The Holy Spirit of God is the only Person that can give us victory over sin, temptation and our flesh, not memorizing scriptures or fasting food (**Romans 8:10-14**).

Believers are Defeated Because of Lack of Knowledge!

Because most Church's do not give detailed teachings to their members on how to handle and have victory over sin, most Christians are being defeated every day in their Christian life, and their walk with God is fearful, unfruitful, confusing and lonely.   Everyday life can be very confusing and lonely for Christians who want to live for God and do His will, but when they look at their own lives and see how they are being defeated by sin and temptation they begin to wonder what is wrong with them.   Not having victory over the sin in their own lives is one of the main reasons why most Christians do not witness to unbelievers. Because they look at their own lives and say to themselves how can I witness to someone else while I am being defeated by sin myself.   How can I help someone else when I can't even help myself?   This is why the Prophet Hosea said in the book of Hosea; **my people are destroyed**

by lack of knowledge (**Hosea 4:6**).   There is only one Pastor that I know of that teaches every day on the subject of having victory over sin, and he lives in Baton Rouge La.   Being taught how to have victory over sin and temptation will bring peace and joy to your Christian life and remove the fear of failure.   Don't get me wrong we all fail it is a part of life, but when failure becomes all you think about because of the sin in your life, then it will begin to control your everyday life and God does not want that to happen to you.   Constant failure can make you depressed, and that can open another door for the devil to come into your life.

By the Grace of God, I am going to try and teach you everything that God has taught me about how to have victory over sin and temptation.   This book is based on what God has taught me, (and is teaching me), and I hope this will help you have more victory over your sins and temptations.   I am not teaching Sinless perfection, because there is no such person, the only Sinless man that ever lived is Jesus Christ our Lord.   Stay away from teachings that teach sinless perfection, because they are false teachings.   In **1 John: 1:8**, God said, **if we say we have no Sin**, we are deceiving ourselves and the truth is not in us.   Sinless perfection teaches that when a person is saved through salvation, that they do not have to ask God for forgiveness any more when they sin again, because all of our sins are covered by the Cross of Christ, (which is true), Jesus did die for all of our sins past, present and future, but we still commit sins every day that affect our walk with God, these sins/trespasses separate us from Him, and this is why we must confess them to Him.   These daily sins, (they are called trespasses in the Lord's Prayer **Luke 11:4 KJV**), must be confessed so we can be forgiven of them, and then we can continue to have a close and personal relationship with God.   **Proverbs 28:13** teaches us that he who covers his sins will not prosper, but whoever confesses and forsakes them will have mercy, and God Himself tells us in **Matthew 6:14-15** that if we do not forgive others of their trespasses (daily sins) against us, then He will not forgive us of our trespasses (daily sins) against others.   Remember God is HOLY and His Eyes are pure, and any sin that we commit will separate us from Him because He cannot look on sin without judging it

13

(**Habakkuk 1:13, Isaiah 59:2**). And this is why He gave us **1John 1:9**, so we can confess our sins/trespasses to Him, and then God will forgive us of our sins/trespasses so we can continue to have a close and personal relationship with Him. But we must first confess our sins to Him in order to receive the forgiveness we need to walk closely with Him. Another danger that the false teaching of sinless perfection will bring upon believers is the taking of the Lord's Supper in an unworthy manner. Because if you do not confess your sins to God for forgiveness, and you then go to Church and receive the Lord's Supper at communion, you have just taken His Holy Communion in an unworthy manner. And as **1 Corinthians 11:27-30** teaches, verse (**29**) teaches that when you take the Lord's Supper in an unworthy manner you eat and drink judgment to yourself. And verse (**30**) says; for this reason, many are weak and sick among you, and many sleep, or are dead. And verse (**28**) clearly tells everyone to examine yourself before you take Communion, meaning if you have any un-confessed sin or anything in your life that is not pleasing to God, then you should confess it and ask God for forgiveness before you take Communion. So, this is why I said to stay away from people who teach sinless perfection because they are setting themselves up for the judgment of God, and furthermore if anyone tries to tell you that you should live a certain way or you should do this or do that to follow God, then you should tell them that they must explain it to you in detail, and give you a scripture from the Bible, (**in context**), that back's up what they are saying. If they cannot give you a scripture reference from the Bible then do not believe them (**Colossians 2:16-23 and Hebrews 13:8-9**). In this day and time, we must be like the Bereans in **Acts 17:11** and search the scriptures to see if what people are saying is true, and in the Bible. A lot of things that people say are from the Bible are not in the Bible, (for example, God help's those who help themselves is not in the Bible), make them show it to you in a Bible or do not believe them. We must test every spirit, and check out **everything** that a person tries to tell us is from God and in the Bible, as God stated in **1Thessalonians 5:21 and 1John 4:1**, there are many false profits and liars out there, and they will say anything to get you under their control, because believe it or not the Scribes and the Pharisees are still around, (we call them legalist today), preaching false doctrines and trying to get Born Again Believer's to follow the Law.   God has already made this decision over 2000 years ago when He called a special meeting between all of the Apostles and made a decree, (**Acts 15:1-29**), that Born Again Believer's do not have to get circumcised or follow the Law (**Acts 15:8-10,19,20,24,28,29, Galatians 2:16, 3:19-29, 1Timothy 1:9-11**).   1Timothy 1:9-11 teaches us who the law is for, the law is not for a righteous person but for the un-saved/sinners.   Born Again Believers are made righteous through the Cross of Jesus Christ after Salvation, so the law is not for us.   Remember that God wrote the laws found inside the Bible, and we have God the Holy Spirit living inside of us, and He is not going to let us do anything that will cause us to sin against God, He will always try to warn us first when we are about to do something wrong.   If believers would just read their Bibles and check out what people are saying, by looking for it in the Bible, (and in context), then they would see that this person is lying to them.   God has commanded us in the Bible to Study to show ourselves approved (**2Timothy 2:15**), so we should not be fooled by these lying men/women who are teaching these false doctrines, **believers please look up stuff before you believe it**.   There are false teachings by false religions out in the world today that tell you that you must go to church on Saturday only, (the sabbath), and you are sinning if you go to church on Sunday, and some of them try to tell you what you can and cannot eat. Believer's the answers to these lies are in the Bible, the 1st one about only going to church on Saturday, these are the scriptures that teach us that the Apostle Paul met with Believers on the First day of every week, which is Sunday, to worship and handle church business (**Acts 20:7, Romans 14:5-9, 1 Corinthians 16:1-2 and Colossians 2:16, 20-23**), and we know that God our Father approved of the Apostle Paul preaching on Sunday because He did not tell him to stop preaching on the first day of the week, which is Sunday.   If Preaching on Sunday was wrong, then God would have told the Apostle Paul to stop Preaching on Sunday and return to Saturday worship, the Apostle Paul was the man that God used to write most of the New Testament Bible for Him, so I know He would have corrected Paul if he was doing something wrong and against His Will.   And in regards to what foods that we can eat, the Bible teaches us in these scriptures that we can eat whatever we want to eat as long as we give thanks to God for our meals (**1Timothy 4:3-5, Romans 14:1-6, 14-23, 1 Corinthians 10:23-33, Colossians 2:16, 20-23**).   We are not required to follow the diet that God gave to the Jews in the Old Testament, you can if you want to that's up to you, but you cannot judge others who do not as being sinners are unhealthy. **1Timothy 4:3-5** teaches us that **we can eat whatever we want to eat** as long as we give thanks to God for our meals, verse (**4**) For every creature of God is Good, and nothing is to be refused if it is received with thanksgiving; (**5**) for it is sanctified by the word of God and prayer. Now if your Doctor tells you not to eat certain foods because it is bad for your health and can do you harm, then common sense tells you that you cannot eat that food, so don't.   But don't let people put you under bondage and make you feel bad because of the food you eat, these people are listening to false teachers from false religions who are using food to control them, so do not fall into their trap, go and enjoy your life and the food you eat, that's the way that God would want us to live.   And make sure you double check the things I am telling you with the Word of God also, you do not know me, I could be just another nut out here wanting to write something.   People makeup stuff and lie on God and the Bible all the time just to make money, and most people will believe them instead of comparing what they are saying to what the Bible teaches, believers are not supposed to believe everything they hear, we are supposed to compare everything to the Word of God to see if it is True, like the Bereans in **Acts 17:11**.   The Bible teaches us to check things out first before we believe in them as we are taught in **Ephesians 4:7**; the Bible teaches that believers should not fall for every wind of doctrine composed by the trickery of men.   Just because someone stands up in front of the Church and speaks does not make them a man/woman of God, satan has people he has planted in every Church to keep up confusion and to miss inform the people of God, just as satan himself sometimes appears as an angel of light to fool and lead people away from God and the Bible, his followers do the same (**Matthew 13:24, 25, 37-39 and 2Corinthians 11:14-15**).   So please check out **everything** someone tries to tell you is from God, because in **2 Timothy 3:13-15** God teaches us that evil men and impostors will grow worse and worse as the return of Christ gets closer, deceiving many and being deceived, so please be on guard to what you hear and believe, (**check it out first**), because people will try to deceive you (**1 John 2:26**).

    I am not a Pastor nor a Sunday school teacher, I am just a regular church member like yourself. I am only writing this message because the Lord has placed this teaching in my heart to write to you, and because I am trying to say no to the sin in my life also, this book is based on what God has taught me so far. The information in this book is not what I have heard someone else teach or experience, this information comes from my own personal life experiences, straight from the horse's mouth. When God began to give me the burden in my heart to write this message, I was being defeated by sin constantly. And I felt like He had chosen the wrong person for this job because I saw no victory over the sin in my life. None at all, I mean, know where, every time I was tempted by sin I gave in, so I did not understand why He choose me. And I did not want to write this message and then turn right around and fall into sin again and embarrass Him, the Lord Jesus Christ and the Holy Spirit. And secondly, I hate to write, the only time that you will see me pick up a pencil or pen is because I have too. Thirdly, I told God that there are already so many good pastors out there that preach the Gospel and have good reputations that people will listen to and follow, and these pastors will do a better job of writing this message than I will. But God would not leave me alone, every day He put thoughts in my mind about how to say no to sin. I understand why now because deep down inside of my heart this was my desire also, I wanted to stop sinning against Him all the time. As a Christian I felt like I should be able to say no to sin sometime, I should not give into sin every time I am tempted by it. So, I knew that something was wrong with me, and I also knew that the answer to my sin problem was in the Bible, I just did not know where in the Bible to look. So, I prayed to God and I said to Him that I did not want to write this message if I could not live it myself, and from that day until now He has been teaching me how to have victory over my sins. And I have learned everything that I am writing to you from HIM, (God the Father), through the Holy Spirit, and I Thank You God my Father for teaching me and for being patient with me by forgiving me when I have sinned against you.

I know you have heard of or might even know of someone that was addicted to drugs or alcohol and then they gave their life to Jesus Christ and was set free from those bad habits and they never did them again.   So, I always wondered why I was not able to walk away from my sins, because I was saved just like they were saved, I gave my life to Jesus Christ too, so I knew there was something I was missing, and I had to find out what it was.   I knew the answers to my questions were in the Bible, and I also knew that only God could show me where the answers were because I had looked all over the place for books and teachings on how to have victory over sin and temptation, but I could not find anything on the subject.   Then one day I heard a pastor on Christian radio teach on Romans: 6,7 and 8, and he said if you understand Romans: 6, then you will live like Romans: 8, and if you do not understand Romans 6, then you will live like Romans: 7, that message started my journey into the book of Romans.   Because deep down inside of me I knew the answer to my sin problem was there, inside the book of Romans chapters 5,6,7,8.   And now many years have passed since God began to teach me how to say no to my sins and temptations. I have fallen many times in my trials against sin and temptation, but each and every time the Lord has forgiven me, and then He would pick me up and dust me off and then pushed me back out there into the battle against sin and temptation to fight some more, until I started to learn what to do, (**You Pray to God for Help**), and you must fully understand what Jesus's death on the Cross has already done for us (Born Again Believers/Christians).   I am not afraid anymore to battle with sin, because I now know that God is in control of everything and that He is always with me in any situation that I might find myself in, whether good or bad.   Now, I still sin and struggle with sin, and you will sin again also.   Sin is one thing we will struggle with until the day we die because sin is inside of us, inside our flesh, and it will always try to control us (**Galatians 5:17, James 3:2 and 1 John 2:1-2**).   But, because God is teaching me how to have victory over my sins and temptations, I now have more peace and joy in my everyday life.   I hope the information that I am about to give you bring more victory over your sins and temptations and give you the peace and joy that can only come from Almighty God Himself. Some of you might not need this message, I am sure there are some Pastors out there that are teaching messages on how to say no to sin.   But if you travel a lot for work as I do and you cannot go to Sunday school or church every Sunday, or you have not been taught how to have victory over sin and temptation, then this message is for you.   As I stated earlier that I searched all over for books and messages on how to have victory over sin and temptation but I could not find anything to help me, and this is why I am writing this book, and I encourage other Christians to write on the subject also. And I hope and pray that every Church that preaches the Gospel of Jesus Christ will have a Sunday School class that teaches the members of that Church the principles of how to have victory over sin and temptation, and I think that all Pastors should teach on the subject at least 4 times a year or more.   The more information and instruction we have on the subject should help Born Again Believers to begin to have more victory over their sins.   Being taught how to have victory over your sins is information that all Born Again Believers will use every day in their Christian life.   I cannot explain to you how good it feels to wake up every morning and not worry about how I will mess up and sin against God again today, because I cannot say no to my sin and temptations. God has taught me, (and is teaching me), that through the renewing of my mind with His Holy Word the Bible, and by praying to the Holy Spirit for help when I am tempted to sin, that I can say no to my sins and temptations.

A Good and Clear Conscience

Because of salvation through the Cross of Jesus Christ, we now have a good and clear conscience with God **(1Peter 3:21)**.   When Adam and Eve sinned against God in the Garden of Eden, they received an evil conscience from sin when it entered their bodies, and this evil conscience was passed down to every living creature on earth, human beings as well as animals.   This evil conscience, (bent toward sin), and sin itself will continue to control every man and woman until the day they die if they do not return to God for help that they need, and this help can only be received through salvation, coming through the Cross of

19

Jesus Christ, being Born Again and being filled with the Holy Spirit of God.   But thanks be to God because when Jesus Christ died on the Cross for all of our sins, His blood also gave us a good and clear conscience toward God again, and the power to say no to sin (**Hebrews 9:14, 10:22, 1 Peter 3:21 and Romans 6:12-14**).

A Clear conscience in your everyday life with God and others means;

1. you have asked God to forgive you of all your daily sins/trespasses, and you know He has forgiven you because of the Cross of Christ and **1 John 1:9**, and
2. There is no other person that you know of that you have offended and owe an apology to.
3. No more Guilty Feelings and the weight that they carry.

A clear conscience with God and man will guide you into experiencing the peace that surpasses all understanding, and having and enjoying this peace all day long (**Philippians 4:4-7**).   This is one of the benefits you will enjoy when you begin to have victory over your sin.   Turning your entire life over to God is the best thing that a Born Again Believer can do, I cannot explain to you my everyday feelings of peace and joy that I have received from God after I gave Him my whole life.   I can truly say that **Matthew 11:28-30** is true.

Matthew 11:28-30; and **Jesus said come to me**, all you who labor and are heavy laden, **and I will give you rest**. (**29**) Take my yoke upon you **and learn from Me**, for I am gentle and lowly in heart, **and you will find rest for your souls**. (**30**) **For my yoke is easy** and **My burden is light**.

I am not saying that I don't have some rough days, because we all do, but what I am saying is that they are few and far in between.   And even when I am having a rough day with sin and temptation, I know that God is there with me, so when things really get rough, I just stop what I am doing, and I pray to God for the help and strength that I will need to endure my temptations and to give me victory over them, and He has never let me down.   I hope that what you are about to read will help you with your sin problem also, and I pray that the peace that comes from God will release off of you all of the guilt and pressure that comes from sin so that you can live for God the way you should.   Pray to God when you need help, because He loves you, and He will help you.   And remember to only believe God and the Bible and not men/women. Please Look Up and Check Everything Out before you Believe it. Amen!

CHAPTER TWO

God is in Control

Acts 17:25-27 states that God **(25) gives to all life, breath and all things**. **(26)** And He has made from **one blood every nation of men** to dwell on all the face of the earth, and has determined their **pre-appointed times and the boundaries of their dwellings, (27)** so they should **seek the Lord**, in the hope that they might grope for Him **and find Him,** though He is not far from each one of us;

The Bible verse above teaches us that God made every human being from the same batch of blood and that He determines;
1. Where on the earth everyone will be born, and
2. How long each one of us will live.

And God does this so we can find Him and the Lord Jesus Christ for Salvation because without His help none of us would have found the Them.

So, let us start with first things first, God is in control of everything and everybody on Planet Earth, and the Bible is the true Word of God.   This is a decision you must make up in your mind right now and believe it in your heart before we can go any further.   Because, if it is hard for you to believe that God is in control of everything in your life and the world around you, then you will be defeated by sin and satan time and time again.   So, you now must make up your mind, right now today, and believe that God is in control of everything in this world, and if God said it then it is true, no questions asked!   Even if you do not see any evidence of what God has stated coming true in your life, just believe it, because Jesus said that God's Word is Truth (**John 17:17**). And if you are a Born Again Christian, then you should see some evidence of God working in your life, if you have food to eat, a place to stay and clothes on your back, then you should be content (**1 Timothy 6:6-8**).   God promised to give us the things we need not the junk we want, (if you seek first the kingdom of God), so be content with the things that you have (**Matthew 6:31-34, Hebrews 13:5-6**). As you grow closer to God and the Lord Jesus Christ, the evidence of God's interventions on your behalf will show up in your life, and then you will begin to see and understand things you did not in the past.   This will also be your foundation to stand on when good or bad things happen in your life, even things you do not understand.   You must understand that if God allowed something to happen to you in your life, (whether good or bad), He allowed it for a reason, it will either benefit you, someone around you or it will teach you a lesson.   Either way, the incident will draw you closer to God and Christ, and then you will learn to depend on them when things happen in your life instead of yourself or others.

The Bible states in **Numbers 23:19** that **God** is not a man, **that He should lie**, and in **Hebrews 6:18** that **it is impossible** for **God** to **Lie**, and in **Titus 1:2 God, who cannot Lie**, so if God cannot lie as these scriptures teach, then this means that everything written in the Bible is True, because the Bible is the inspired Word of God (**2 Timothy 3:16-17**).   When you are **fully convinced**, (meaning you really believe, without a shadow of doubt that what God has said is true), that you can believe and trust God, and you believe that He is in total control of everything in your life and the world around you and that everything He has spoken in the Bible is true, then and only then will you stop trying to run your life your way and give your whole life over to God so He can control it His way.   Our lives are in His hands and whatever happens to us must come through Him for approval.   This will also make it easy for you to cast all of your cares and worries upon Him because God truly loves and cares for us (**1Peter 5:7**), and in **Jeremiah 29:11-13** God tells us how He has good and loving thoughts towards us.

Jeremiah 29:11-13; (**11**) For I know the thoughts that I think towards you says the Lord, thoughts of peace and not of evil, to give you a future and a hope.   (**12**) Then you will call upon Me and go and pray to Me, and I will listen to you.   (**13**) And you will seek Me and find Me, when you search for Me with all of your heart.

A couple of my favorite scriptures are **Romans 8:31 and Hebrews 13:5-6,** they teach us that; **Romans 8:31** if God is for us, then who can be against us, and **Hebrews 13:5-6** for He Himself has said, be content with what you have because I will never leave you nor forsake you, **(6)** so we may boldly say: The Lord is my helper, I will not fear. What can man do to me?

Take some time and just think about what **Romans 8:31** and **Hebrews 13:5-6** are trying to teach us. Who can defeat God..., **No One!!!** So, why do we worry when things we do not understand happen to us, it is only natural to worry when something has just happened to us, but after we have had time to think about the situation, we should just turn it over to God in prayer and not worry about it anymore. We should just pray to God about it and then just watch to see how He solves the problem for us His way. If you are a child of God, (meaning, you are a Born Again Christian), then He will take care of you, He promises us this in **Matthew 6:31-34** and **Romans 8:28** because He is our Father and He is on our side if we follow and keep His commandments. And the commandments Jesus gave us to follow are **(1)** to love God with all of your heart, your mind and your soul and **(2)** to love your neighbor as yourself. As Jesus said in (**Matthew 22:35-40, Mark 12:28-31 and Luke 10:27-28**) if you will just keep these two commandments, you will fulfill the whole book of the law. And remember, this is not our battle any way it is Gods, and He has already defeated Satan and sin over 2000 years ago at the Cross of Jesus Christ our Lord and Savior **(Colossians 2:13-15).** I know what you are going to say but look at what has happened to me in my life, yes, I know some really bad things have happened to some of us. We all have been through something in our lives that we did not like or understand, but we must understand that God allowed those things to happen to all of us for a reason:

1. To draw us to Him and Jesus for help and,
2. For God to use us to help someone else who is going through what we went through **(2 Corinthians 1:3-4).**

God could have prevented those things from happening to me and you, but He did not, because He knew we would make it through, and because He has plans for us, because everything that we have experienced in our lives, whether good or bad, will prepare us for the job God has in store for us.   This is why He needs us just as we are, with all of our mistakes and failures, God still can use us to help someone else find Him, (yes), He needs someone just like me and you just the way we are.   For example, in the book of Job (**Job chapter's 1, 2**), in Job's life, Satan could not do anything to Job without God's permission.   Everything that happened to Job God allowed, and while Job was going through his trials, he did not understand what was happening to him.   But later, after he went through his trials, God gave him the understanding that he needed.   And God works the same way in believer's lives today, satan must have permission from God before he can do anything to a Born Again Believer.   For example, in **Luke 22:31-32** Jesus told Peter that satan had requested to shift him like wheat, and then God allowed the devil to test Peter, and Peter denied knowing Jesus 3 times that same night.   So, look back over your life and the trials in your life, and try to learn from them, and then ask God to help you understand what happened and why, He will give you the answer you seek.   Most believers do not like the answer that God gives us because most of the time there was something that we did to cause the problem in the first place, (Sins against God will lead to punishment), and then we always say I don't understand why this has happened to me.   I know that sometimes other people do things that affect us and we had nothing to do with it, and we suffer because of their actions, and then some people are angry because they have disabilities that they were born with, and I understand that, but you must remember that disabilities that we were born with came from God, and He allowed us to be born that way for His Purpose **Exodus 4:11**.   But, for most of us our troubles can be traced back to our sins.   People are always saying why do bad things happen to good people?   First of all, (there are no good people), God has said that we are all sinners and deserve to go to hell, so when bad things happen to bad people, (it is because it is supposed to), because we are all sinners (**Romans 3:9-20**).   Everything that happens in this world, (good or bad), happens so it can lead us to God and Christ.   But when some type of evil happens to a child it always breaks my heart and I never understood why, so I asked God why and He said because most people don't believe that I am real, so when they see some kind of evil thing that has happened to a child, then they realize that evil does exists, and then they will realize that **I AM**.   Because if evil exists then there must be good somewhere also, and they know that evil comes from the devil, and then they will realize that good comes from **Me, GOD**.   Whenever something happens to anyone in this world, (whether good or bad), God knows about it, nothing surprises Him, because He knew that you would grow up without a father/mother, and He knew you would be a single parent and He knows who will get divorced and who will lose their child at a young age, and I could go on and on, but I think you get the message.   So please just go to God with all of your worries and cares because He is there in Heaven just waiting for us to call on Him in prayer so that He can comfort us.   And please be prepared to witness to and help people who have been through situations similar to yours, because God will be sending them in your life.   God has prepared you just for these people, and you just might be the only person that can see their pain and understand what they are going through, they are crossing your path for a reason.   So please be ready to help them anyway you can, because they will really need someone just like you, someone who understands and can relate to their situation **(2Corinthians 1:3-4)**.

A Picture of the Rapture

Sunday March 22, 2020, was the **First time** in the History of the Church of God and Jesus Christ where Almost **Every Church** All Around the Whole World was Closed for Worship Service to God and Christ because of the coronavirus.   Some churches did do video messages and live streaming but that is different from church members meeting together and worshiping and praising God and Jesus Christ together as a family/group as God commands us in **Hebrews 10:25**. There was No praising and worshiping of God by the members of these churches on this day, only closed up buildings standing across the land empty and vacant.   On the Day when Billions of men/women are scheduled to Always worship God and Jesus Christ and sing songs of Glory to them, the Heavens were Silent. I am sure some True believers did worship and go to Church, but the rest of the Churches of Jesus Christ were closed, and this Sunday was not business as usual. I was very upset that my Church was closed also just like all of the rest of them because of the fear of the Coronavirus. I understand the fear that people have concerning this virus because people are dying from it, but that is no reason for the church not to gather together and worship God and Jesus Christ, if anything this is the time that we really need to be coming together inside of the House of God and Praying to Them for help, because Only God and Jesus Christ can cure you from a virus that has No cure. **James 5:14-16** teaches us that If you are sick, then you should call or go to the Elders of the Church and let them Pray over you, and then anoint you with oil in the name of Jesus Christ, and the prayer of faith will save the sick. Listen to me, if you are in the House of God then you are protected by God, Jesus Christ and the Holy Spirit, so if anything happens to you it must be allowed by Almighty God Himself. Remember Born Again/Saved Christians are His Children, so this means that He loves us and He's going to take good care of us, so He is not going to let anything happen to us inside of His House the Church. When we gather together and go to church to serve and worship God we are at home, our real home, we are standing in the presence of God our Father, Our Lord and Savior Jesus Christ and the Holy Spirit of God who is always with us because He is inside of us. **Matthew 18:20** teaches us that if 2 or 3 come together in my name then I am in the midst of them, this means that when we as Born Again/Saved believers meet together for worship either inside of the church or outside of the church that God is there with us, so if He is there with us then what can happen to us. So let me make this as clear to you as possible, if God cannot protect you inside of His house the Church while you are worshipping Him, then He cannot protect you at your house where you are locked up and in hiding, it's just that simple. **Hebrews 9:27** teaches us that God determines when and how everyone will die not the coronavirus, so if God says it is not your time to die then you are not going to die it is just that simple. Now everything I just told you is for Born Again/Saved Believers, the real Children of God, these promises are not for un-believers, fake Christians and followers of false religions, you might get sick and die if you go to your religious meetings, so you better stay in the house and hide unless you give your life to Jesus Christ and get saved. And I know that the government had said that it was not safe to be in a gathering where there will be 10 people of more for fear of catching the virus, but after I left the closed church on Sunday March 22, 2020, I went to a popular department store and it was full of people, at least 200 individuals are more. Wait a minute, I thought the government said that it was not safe to be in a gathering of 10 people are more because of the virus and if so then this place should be closed also, there were stores open all over the place and people going in and out of them except for the House of God the Church of Jesus Christ, so it is ok to go shopping at a store during the virus but it is not safe to go to Church. So, after witnessing this double standard, I was upset and drove home for the rest of the day, but that night I could not go to sleep the thoughts of the Church of God and Jesus Christ being closed continued to stay on my mind all night long and I did not understand why. The next day, Monday March 23, 2020, I asked God why am I still thinking about the churches being closed, and that is when the Holy Spirit said to me not just your church but churches All around the World, All were closed down and empty, there was no worship to God and Christ coming from these houses of God, and there were no followers of Jesus Christ inside of these buildings who could pray for someone if they came by seeking God and Jesus Christ. The Holy Spirit said to me that This is a Picture of the Rapture to Come, He then helped me to understand that in the future when the Rapture of the church happens that the people of the world will see empty churches standing all over the world again, but the difference will be that when this happens again in the future that there will be no followers of Jesus Christ on Earth that they can talk to, un-believers can find someone now that they can talk to about God and Christ, but when the real Rapture happens the people of God will be removed from the Earth and there will be no one that they will be able to talk to about God. Everything happening now is under the control of God for this reason, even the virus, God is sending a message to the Church of Jesus Christ to let them know that The Rapture of the church will happen and that the church of Jesus Christ needs to stay busy preaching the Gospel and saving the lost, and He is also sending a message to un-believers, God is letting them know that today is the day of Salvation and you need to give your life to Jesus Christ today and get Born Again/Saved because you might be sick and dying tomorrow, God is letting them know that they cannot wait and think that they can come to Him whenever they want to and get Saved on their time table. God is letting everybody know that they cannot take the Church of Jesus Christ for granted anymore because it will not always be here for you to run to in time of need. So to keep believers busy God has evicted the members of His church back out into the world because of their lack of faith in Him concerning the coronavirus, they closed down the houses of God because they had more faith in the coronavirus getting to them and making them sick than they had in the Power of God protecting them from it. The faith of the church was tested and the people of the church failed the test, satan asked God if he could sift His church as wheat, (just like he did to Peter in **Luke 22:31-34,** when Peter denied Jesus 3 times), and God said yes to the devil's request to sift the church, and then the coronavirus showed up in the world and the churches of God closed down in fear of the virus, when they closed down they denied the Power of the God that they say they believe in and serve, all because of the fear of getting sick and dying. No matter how you try to explain it to the un-believing world this shows a lack of faith in the Power of God, Jesus Christ and the Holy Spirit who lives inside of Born Again Believers. This is the same thing that happened to the profit Elijah in the old testament in **1Kings 19:1-16** when God fired him **for lack of faith** and Peter in the new testament, people cannot talk about Peter anymore saying how could he deny Jesus Christ like that because if your church closed it's doors like mine did, then you just denied Him also. Peter realized what he had done and went away crying but most believers today do not even realize what they have done and the message that they have sent to the un-believing world. Just like Elijah the members/people of the church of Jesus Christ have closed down the Houses of God and are now in hiding in fear for their lives, just like Elijah they have forgotten All of the Powerful Miracles listed in the Bible as well as Miracles of Healings that God has done throughout the ages and during their life times, and just like Elijah God is asking His church **What are you doing here** in hiding (**1Kings 19:9-16**) after All that I have done for you.   And just like in Elijah's case God is going to speak to His Pastors and tell them to re-open His Churches to show their faith in Him and His Son Jesus Christ, and if they do not, then God will **Fire/remove** people from His church just like He did to Elijah in **1Kings 19:16**.

The church is always preaching that during a crisis that the church of Jesus Christ must show it's faith in God so that the un-believers living around us can see our faith in God which will let them know that God is real, and that He is real in our lives and we believe in and trust Him. Well the crisis is here and where is the church of Jesus Christ, closed down and in hiding just like the un-believers.   I know what some of you are going to say that the church is not a building, I know that and you know that because we have been taught this in the church, but the un-believers do not know this, they look at the church buildings as the house of God and not the people, so when they see that the houses of God are closed down and the people of God are in hiding just like them, then they are not going to believe that God is real, because they are watching our actions and our response to this crisis, and our actions will speak louder to them than our words, so what do you think the un-believers think of us now.

My faith is in God, Jesus Christ and the Holy Spirit and I know that They have a plan to fix all of this and to restore Glory and Honor to Their Names, so since God has kicked all Born Again Believers out of His church and back into the world because of lack of faith, we need to do the Lord's work until He lets us back inside of His church. Believers need to be praying to God to lead people to Salvation, preaching the Gospel of Jesus Christ and we need to be ready to be used by God when He calls upon us to heal, save, pray for and help someone who is in need, because there is no cure for this virus, and people are getting sick and dying every day.   The only cure will be healings Done by God, either through the sending of a vaccine are by using the Elders of His church (**James 5:14-16**) are by 2 or 3 Born Again Believers praying over someone (**Matthew 18:20**), God will get the Glory and

Honor for ending this pestilence.   The coronavirus is a Pestilence as taught to us by Jesus Christ over 2000 years ago in **Matthew 24:3-8**, He knew it was coming so He warned us about it.   So what we are really witnessing with these disasters is the Bible coming True right before our eyes during our lifetime, and this is a good learning lesson for the church, so when events like this happen again true believers should look for it inside of the Bible, the True Word of God, to see what God has to say about it and not get all of your information from un-believers.   You have to remember that the knowledge of how to create a vaccine is given to a person by God, and until God is ready to give that knowledge to someone the whole world must look to Him for help and healing.   Born Again Saved Christians can return to church and resume the worship of God and Jesus Christ because they are the children of God and He promises to protect them, but un-saved people cannot because you have not given your life to Jesus Christ so you are not a Christian and you will be in danger of contracting the virus and getting sick.   False teachers and fake Christians you cannot fake it anymore, God is using this virus crisis to show the world who is a real Christian and who is not.   And remember to only believe God and the Bible not men/women, and Please Check Everything Out before you Believe it.   Amen!

CHAPTER THREE

Sin Where Did It Come From?

Genesis 2:16-17; And the Lord commanded the man, saying, "Of every tree of the garden you may freely eat; but of the tree of the knowledge of good and evil you shall not eat, for in the day that you eat of it you shall surely die."

    Sin entered the world when Adam and Eve disobeyed God in the Garden of Eden and ate from the tree of good and evil (**Genesis 3:6-7**). From this one act of disobedience by Adam and Eve sin entered the world and became a part of man's nature, giving him and every living thing on the earth an evil conscience toward God (**Romans 5:12, Hebrews 10:22**). Then God's Spirit departed from inside of Adam because sin had separated him from God (**Isaiah 59:2**) and Adam became a man with a body, a soul bent towards evil (an evil conscience) and a dead spirit (a spirit not connected to God). Because of Adams's sin the Holy Spirit departed from his body, and every man/woman that has been born since then have been born with a dead spirit and an evil conscience toward the things of God, and this is why a non-believer, (non-Christian, un-saved, not born again person), will never be able to please God, it doesn't matter how hard they try or what they try to do they will never be able to please Him until they give their lives to Jesus Christ and become Born Again and filled with the Holy Spirit of God (**Romans 8:5-7**). And sin, (which is inside of us), will continue to control every man/woman until the day they die if they do not return to God for the help that they need. Salvation, (the forgiveness of our sins), coming through the Cross of Jesus Christ is the **Only Way** that mankind can return to God so that He can help them with their sin and temptation problem, and then they will be able to please God and live for Him as they should. God's desire is to have a relationship with men /women, that's why He created us, and we will never be complete without a relationship with Him. God has placed inside of every man/woman a longing to be re-united to Him, this is the empty feeling that every man/woman has inside of them which makes them feel incomplete or as if they are missing something in their life.   That longing or empty feeling can only be filled by God; our spirit being re-connected to God through His Holy Spirit Whom Born Again Believers receive at salvation.   No person, place or thing, (not money, other people, things or drugs), can satisfy that empty feeling that is inside of every man/woman, only God can satisfy and fulfill that empty feeling.   So, every man/woman must return to God to feel complete, (like Adam and Eve did before they sinned in the Garden of Eden), and to enjoy true happiness in their life.   There is no true happiness in life without a relationship with God and Jesus Christ.

The Apostle Paul recognized that sin was inside of him in (**Romans 7:17, 20, and 23**) when he was writing about the struggle that all believers will have with the sin that is in their flesh.   When he said "but sin that dwells in me", he was letting all of us know that sin still dwells inside a Born Again Believer after Salvation, and that we will have an inside battle as well as an outside battle with sin for as long as we live here on planet earth, and **Galatians 5:17** teaches us this reality also.

Galatians 5:17; For the flesh lusts against the Spirit, and the Spirit against the flesh; and these are contrary to one another, so that you do not do the things that you wish.

Every living thing on earth, (since Adams disobedience), has been controlled by sin, (except Jesus Christ our Lord).   If we know that sin is in the world and affecting every living thing, (both man and nature), then we must learn how to control it, because we going to be tempted by it until the day we die (**Romans 8:20-23, Galatians 5:17**).   So now we must choose how we are going to deal with sin, either with God and the Holy Spirits help, (who was given to us through salvation), or without Them.   As God said to Cain in **Genesis 4:6-7**; why are you angry? And why has your countenance fallen?   If you do well, will you not be accepted?   And if you do not do well, **sin lies at the door**, and **its desire is for you, but you should rule over it**.   We as Born Again

Believer's in God and Christ do not have to look for sin, sin is looking for us, God teaches us in **1Peter 5:8-9**, that satan roams around like a roaring lion looking for someone to devour, and because we are the children of God down here on earth trying to do His will satan will be coming after us. And without God on our side we will be the people getting devoured by satan, so please listen to me, you do not want to battle sin and satan without God and Jesus Christ's help, there is no way you will win, sin and satan are to strong and powerful for you to try and handle without Their help. I am telling you from my own personal experience, I have never had victory over satan and sin until I turned my whole life over to God and Christ, and you won't either. Just look at the history of mankind and use it as a track record against sin and temptation, in every case mankind loses without God's help. From Adam to Noah mankind had no rules, because mankind thought that they were smart enough to govern themselves without God, (and God allowed them to **Acts 14:16**), but mankind under estimated the power of sin and temptation controlled by satan and the outcome was that mankind became so evil that God had to destroy every living thing except for Noah and his family (**Genesis 6:5-8 and 11**). And then God gave Moses the law, (rules to follow /The knowledge of Good and Evil **Genesis 3:6-7**), so that man would know what God considered right and wrong because He wanted man to know what it would take to please Him. And instead of man looking at the laws of God and realizing within himself that there is no way that he could meet these requirements without God's help, (mankind once again), tried to meet the requirements of the law without God's help and failed again. So, from the beginning of time, before the earth was formed, God knew all of this would happen and this is why He sent Jesus Christ His Only Begotten Son into the world to save mankind from sin and satan, and to reconcile men/women back to Himself through the forgiveness of their sins, which **Only** comes through the Cross of Jesus Christ, His death, burial and resurrection (**2 Corinthians 6:17-21 and Colossians 1:14, 20-22**).

God sent Jesus Christ, (down from Heaven), to save us from satan, sin and temptation, and to teach us that we will never have victory over them without Him. Listen to me, If Jesus Christ the Son of GOD had to

34

get up off of His throne in Heaven where He was Loved and Glorified by all, to come down here to planet earth to save us from sin and satan, then this means that we were/are in some big trouble, trouble that we cannot handle ourselves without GOD's help, and the sooner we realize this the better it will be for us.   Some of you might understand what I am talking about, have you ever had a child or relative of yours to call you for help after they had gotten themselves in trouble and then you had to stop what you were doing, take off work to go to where they were at to get them out of trouble because you realized that they could not handle the trouble that they have gotten themselves in, this is the same thing that Jesus had to do for us.   We were/are in deep trouble, satan and sin are trying to take over the world, but thanks be to God and Jesus we now have a chance to say no to sin and yes to God through Salvation.   As Peter stated in **Acts 2:22** when Jesus was here on earth, He proved to everyone that He was sent from God by the miracles, wonders, and signs He performed right before their eyes.   And Jesus also demonstrated His power over satan and his demons by casting them out of people every time He encountered someone who was demon possessed (In all four gospels).   The miracles and acts of power performed by Jesus over sickness and diseases, satan and his demons, once again demonstrates to mankind that we cannot have victory over these things without God's help.   Satan, sin and temptation are just to strong and powerful for any man/woman to handle without God's help, and they are not going anywhere until God has judged them, they will be here fighting against us until the day we die, and sadly enough they will also be here waiting for the next generation of Christians also so that they can try to tempt and control them too.   So, if we really want to help ourselves and the future generations of believers that will follow us, then we should pray to God and ask Him to teach us everything that we will need to know about having victory over our sins and temptations so that we can live to please Him, and then teach the next generation of believers how to do the same. Whether we like it or not, sin and temptation are here to stay and the best thing for Born Again Believers to do is to go to God and pray to Him and ask Him to teach us how to prevent sin and temptation from controlling us in our everyday life, because as God told Cain in **Genesis 4:6-7**; **sins desire is for you**, but you **should rule over it**.   Sin also desires to rule

35

over us, and it will if we do not go to God for help, because if you are trying to do things your way, then you are just like Cain and sin will rule over you, (you will do things that you don't want to do **Romans 7:15-21**), but if you turn to God for help, then He will deliver you from sins grip and then help you live for Him the way you should (**Romans 6:1-22 and 8:1-17**).

Racism is A Sin

There is only One Race of People on Planet Earth in God's Eyes and that is the Human Race (**Acts 17:24-27**).

Acts 17:26-27 And He has made from **One Blood** Every Nation of Men/Women to dwell on all the face of the Earth, and has determined their pre-appointed times and the boundaries of their dwellings, **(27)** so that they should seek the Lord, in the hope that might grope for Him and find Him, though He is not far from each one of us;

Racism is One of the most dangerous sins that is being committed in Society today. It is Dangerous because most people do not know that it is a sin. Most Pastors inside of the Church never preach about it, so most people just think that racism is something that was taught to someone by their parents and that there is nothing that they can do about it. No this is not true, Racism is a sin, even though it was taught to a child or an adult by their parents or by someone else, they still can be changed through the Cross of Jesus Christ. Just like every other sin that's being practice in the world today, racism can be found inside of the Church of Jesus Christ also. You see it every Sunday morning when you go to Church or watch it on T.V., most churches are segregated by race. And you also see it even when you go to Christian conferences, depending on who is giving the event most of the speakers will be of one race or nationality. Racism is being displayed every day in our society from racist police officers shooting unarmed men/women based on their race, to elected official's making policies that affect other people based on their race or country of origin. All of these racist actions are sins against God, and He will punish the people who commit these sins.   Society and the judicial system might try to overlook these sins but the Almighty God of Heaven and earth will not, He does not let any type of sin go un-punished (**Colossians 3:25**), and He promises us in **Galatians 6:7-9** that He will not be mocked, you will reap what you sow, and He is going to make sure that you do.   As I stated in the beginning of this message, most people do not think that racism is a sin but the Bible teaches us **in James 2:9** that if you show partiality/favoritism, you commit sin.   And Racism is showing partiality/favoritism for one race are nationality of people over another race are nationality of people.   Whether it is Black over White or Jewish over Palestinian, it is still Racism/ prejudice and it is a sin in God's Eyes.   The Bible teaches us in **Ephesians 2:14-22** that Jesus's death on the Cross brought together all men/women as one family of believers, to those who trust in Him for their Salvation, making them sisters and brothers in the House of God which is the Church of Jesus Christ, no matter what race are nationally they might be.   Inside of His Holy Word the Bible God makes it very clear that He does not show any partiality towards no man/woman He treats everyone the same (**Acts 10:34-36, Romans 10:12, Galatians 2:6, Ephesians 6:9 and Colossians 3:25**).   Jesus Christ died on the Cross for all men/women regardless of their skin color or country of origin.   Pay close attention to who is approving of are trying to explain away these racist acts that are going on in society today, the people that approve of them or are trying to explain away the seriousness of these racist acts are not Christians, and are not of God.   No matter who they are pastor's, president, congress person's, radio and news outlets, these people are not of God, but they are being used by the devil to spread hate and division, so they can kill, steal and destroy other people's lives.   Through these racist acts God is showing the world who are Christians and who are not Christians, so pay close attention to and remember these people and organizations who are approving of these racist acts, do not follow them or give money to their causes, because they are using Christianity and the name of God and Jesus Christ to make money and to gain influence in the world.   These people and organizations do not care about God or Jesus Christ, all they care about is money and power, so they will say that they are Christians knowing that most Christians will believe them, and they will allow some preaching of the Gospel on their radio and T.V. stations in the morning or late at night just to make it seem like they are a Christian station, while the majority of the broadcasts on these stations are political, racist and evil, they spread false news leading to divisions among the people who listen to them and the followers of God and Christ. They do this to fool gullible Christians or people who think that they are Christians, people who do not read and study their Bibles, because if they did, then they would know that these radio, T.V. stations and news outlets are not of God. Born Again Believers, **WAKE UP**, and please remember what Jesus taught us in **Matthew 15:18-20 and Mark 7:20-23,** that **whatever comes out of the mouth of a man/woman** comes from inside their heart, and the things that they say will show you who they really are, Good or Evil, Born Again/Saved or un-saved, so listen and pay close attention to what people around you are saying. If you just listen and pay close attention to what kind of information that these radio, T.V. stations and news outlets are prod casting, then you will notice that all of the information that you will hear are the works of the flesh **Galatians 5:19-21**, hatred, contentions, dissensions, outbursts of wrath, envy, murders…etc. And as a Child of God and a follower of Jesus Christ we are required to stand up for what is right and Godly, no matter what situation that we might find ourselves in or who is speaking, if we see are hear something that is sinful being done in our presence, then we should say something about it and give Godly Bible based answers to correct the lies of the devil. Because Racism is a Sin.

The Good Samaritan was an Inter-racial Man

A Samaritan is a person with one Jewish parent and one parent of another race/nationality, and this is why the Good Samaritan stopped to help the Jewish man who was hurt, (**1**) he was a good person and he saw someone who was hurt and needed his help, (**2**) he had good Jewish relatives who had loved and treated him good because if his Jewish relatives had treated him badly, he probably would not have stopped to help this injured Jewish man on the side of the road, and this is why Jesus told the Jews the Parable of the Good Samaritan so that the Jews could see that there is good in everyone, no matter what their race or nationality (**Luke 10:25-37**).   Jesus Christ had to deal with racism when He was here on Earth also, the racism being played out between the Jews and the Samaritans, and the gentiles/other races/nationalities.   The Jews did not like the Samaritans and the Samaritans did not like the Jews, all because the Samaritans were inter-racial people from inter-racial marriages, and the Jews hated them for marrying someone of another race/nationality.   And we see this same type of racism against inter-racial couples being played out today all over the world that we live in, from the United States of America to every country on Planet Earth, in every country, there are people who do not want people of different races/tribes/clans to marry and be happy together, because of racism, racism is a global sin.   God does approve of inter-racial marriages today as He did long ago, as long as the person that you marry is a Christian. God teaches us in **2Corinthians 6:14** that we should not be unequally yoked together with an unbeliever, meaning that the person that we chose to marry should be a Christian and not a person of another religion or of no religion.   God commands us not to marry un-believers because they are going to try to get you to follow their religion or lifestyle instead of following God and Jesus Christ, and this is exactly what happened to King Solomon in the Old Testament (**1Kings 11:1-4**).   All of the leaders we read about in the Bible were also in inter-racial marriages, from Abraham to Solomon they all had wives from other nationalities/races (**Genesis11:29, 16:3, 25:1-6, 1Chronicles 1:32-33, Genesis 41:45-52, Exodus 2:21-22, Numbers 12:1, 1Samuel 18:20-25, 2Samuel 3:1-5**).   Miriam Moses sister was punished by God and given leprosy because of Racism; she became angry with Moses because he married and had an Ethiopian wife from Africa (**Numbers 12:1-16.** And Jesus Christ Himself had Samaritans in His family tree, **Boaz was a Samaritan Man**, and then He married Ruth who was a Moabite making their marriage an inter-racial marriage, which made their children Samaritans.   This explains why Boaz was an older man and had never been married, even though he was a good person and wealthy businessman (**Ruth 2:1**), He was a Samaritan, and the Jews living around him would not give one of their daughters in marriage to him, because they were racist toward the Samaritans.   Boaz's father was

Salmon who was Jewish and his mother was Rahab from the city of Jericho, Rahab begot Boaz, Boaz begot Obed by Ruth, Obed begot Jesse, and Jesse begot David the King (**Ruth 4:10-22**, **Matthew 1:5-6**), and in the New Testament, Timothy who followed the Apostle Paul was also a Samaritan (**Acts 16:1**).   And this is probably why Jesus Christ Himself kept traveling through Samaria on His different journeys, (**1**) He had relatives who lived there and (**2**) He was making the Apostles, His disciples and the other people who followed Him around helping Him with His ministry interact with the people of Samaria, so that they could see that they were good people and that they believe in same God that they believed in.   And on one of His journeys through Samaria, He met and talked to a Samaritan woman at one of Jacobs well's, which led to many Samaritans believing that He was the Christ the Savior of the World (**John 4:1-42**).   As I told you earlier Racism is a sin and God will punish you for practicing it whether you are a Christian are not, and especially people inside of His House the Church.   God is going to judge and punish people inside of His Church for practicing Racism because this sin divides the House of God hindering believers from working together to present the Gospel of Jesus Christ to the whole world, and He cannot allow that to happen because this is why we are here to save people from Hell.   Racism is a serious sin that everyone needs to pay close attention to and do not tolerate it from anyone no matter who they are, family are friends.   And as you can see from the history of the Bible that inter-racial couples have been around from the very beginning of time, and they are not going anywhere, so you might as well get use to them.   Because as I stated earlier, **Racism is a Sin,** and God will punish you for practicing it.   And remember to only believe God and the Bible not men/women, and Please Check Everything Out before you Believe it.   Amen!

CHAPTER FOUR

What is A Christian?

John 3:3-8; **And Jesus** told Nic-O-De-Mus, (a ruler of the Jews), "Most assuredly, I Say To You, **Un-less One is Born Again, he Cannot See the Kingdom of God.**"

Matthew 18:3; And Jesus Said Un-Less You are Converted (Becoming Born Again), and become as little children, (By Believing Everything that God has Told You to Believe), **You Will By No Means Enter the Kingdom of Heaven**.

Acts 3:19; Repent therefore and Be Converted (Being Born Again), that your sins may be blotted out, so that times of refreshing may come from the presence of the Lord.

A Christian is someone who is a follower of Jesus Christ and His teachings, someone who believes that Jesus Christ is the Son of God and that He is also God, and that Jesus came into the world to die for the sins of the world so that men/women can receive forgiveness for their sins which will allow them to go to Heaven when they die to live with God forever **(John 1:1-4, 3:16-18)**. A Christian believes that Jesus Christ is the **ONLY WAY** to God and Heaven, (because Jesus Christ Himself said in **John 14:6** that He is the way, the truth, and the life and **No One comes to the Father except through Me**). And a Christian also believes that Jesus's death on the Cross was for the forgiveness for all of their sins, (every sin that they will ever commit), past, present and future. Born Again Christians have put their trust and faith in Jesus's death on the Cross for the forgiveness of their sins which allows them to become children of God, **(Romans 8:14-17 and Galatians 3:26-29 and 4:3-7)**, and gives them entrance into the Grace of God and Eternal Life with God in Heaven. Jesus died on the Cross at Calvary over 2000 years ago, (so all of our sins are future sins compared to when He died), because none of us was living when He lived, so every sin that we will ever commit will be considered a future sin, which means that He has already paid the price for all of our sins past, present and future.   So, let us start at the beginning because most of the people that go to church don't even know what salvation means.

Salvation means to be delivered from sin and its consequences so that someone will be allowed to enter Heaven and live with God.

As the definition above explains you must be forgiven of your sins to be allowed to enter Heaven to live with God and Christ, and the **ONLY** way your sins will be forgiven is through the Cross of Jesus Christ.   God will not accept any other sacrifice for the forgiveness of sin except for the death of His Only Begotten Son, Jesus Christ.   As Peter told the Jews in **Acts 4:12** when he spoke to them about Jesus; he said (Nor is there salvation in any other, for there is no other name under Heaven given among men by which we must be saved), salvation comes through Jesus Christ and Him Only, you cannot work or buy your way into Heaven.   The reason we need Salvation through Jesus Christ is because our sins have separated us from God (**Isaiah 59:2**), and the only way that we can be re-united with Him is through the forgiveness of our sins which comes through the Cross of Jesus Christ.   When Jesus died on the cross His Holy Blood came out of His body to be used by God to cover and forgive our sins which had separated us from God, and this had to happen because God had made a law stating that there will be no forgiveness of sin without the shedding of blood (**Hebrews 9:12-14 and 9:22**).   So, please do not be fooled by all of these other false religions that teach that there are many ways to God and Heaven, they are lying to you, God has told us how to get to Him in Heaven, (**He wrote us a personal letter called the Bible**, and **He has already provided away**, through the Cross of **Jesus Christ** His Only Begotten Son), so that anyone who wants to come to Heaven and live with Him can.   God has written all of this down for us inside His Holy Word the Bible, so please just read the Bible and do what it tells you to do, because if you continue to listen to these false religions and people that say there are many ways to God, and not to Almighty God Himself, then you will die in your sins, and you will then go to Hell.   As Jesus told the Jews in **John 8:24"** If you do not believe that I am He, you will die in your sins", and if you die in your sins, (meaning your sins have not been forgiven by God), then you will go to Hell, (**and it will be your fault**), because God has told us what to do to have our sins forgiven so that we can come and live with Him in Heaven forever.   You must accept God's Free offer for Salvation through His Son Jesus Christ, this is the **Only way** that you can be saved from the punishment of God and not go to Hell.   It is now up to you, are you going to listen to God and believe Him and do what He tells you to do or are you going to continue to listen to these false religions and teachers who contradict the teachings in God's Holy Word the Bible.   Either way, you cannot say that God did not try to warn you and lead you in the right direction.   God is not going to perform something miraculous in the sky to get people to believe in Him, in **1Corinthians 1:21** God said, "I will give them **a simple message** and **those who believe it will be saved**", (and in other words), for those who do not believe His message they will not be saved.

　　1 Corinthians 1:21; For since, in the wisdom of God, the world through wisdom did not know God, **it pleased God through the foolishness of the message preached to save those who believe**.

　　A miracle in the sky will not make most people believe in God and His Holy Word the Bible, there will always be someone who will try to explain it away as something not of God.   Our Lord and Savior Jesus Christ did many miracles during His earthly ministry, and some of the people that witnessed them still refused to repent of their sins and believe in Him.   And Jesus rebuked the inhabitants of these cities for their unbelief (**Matthew 11:20-24**), this proves that miracles alone will not make you believe in God.   The message of the Gospel of Jesus Christ is how God is going to save people from Hell and allow them to come to Heaven to live with Him, so either you believe in God and trust what He has spoken in His Holy Word Bible or you will not be Born Again/Saved, it is just that simple.   God has placed Churches all over the world and on almost every corner in most cities/towns, and the Gospel of Jesus Christ is being preached all over the world and over all types of information mediums.   So, most people cannot say that they have never heard of Jesus Christ, because if you refuse to listen to and believe in the Gospel of Jesus Christ that's being preached from these Churches, then you will not believe a miracle.   This is what Abraham told the rich man in Hades in the story of Lazarus and the rich man in **Luke 16:27-31, in verse 31** Abraham told him that if his family will not listen to Moses and the Prophets, then they will not be persuaded by someone rising from the dead.   And I know what you are going to say next, how is God going to judge **the person who has never heard the Gospel** of Jesus Christ, God will still judge them but in a different way. These people are still covered by the Blood of Jesus Christ and are forgiven of their sins, but they did not know it because the Gospel of Christ did not reach them before they died, so God will judge them based on **Romans 2:14-16**.

   There is one thing that everyone needs to remember, in **Hebrews 9:27** the Bible teaches that God has appointed a day for every man/woman to die, and then **the judgment**.   The very second that you die you will know if you are going to Heaven or to Hell, this is **the judgment**, Christians (Born Again Believers), will go to Heaven to live with God and Christ, (inside of their Heavenly Bodies, which are now in Heaven **2 Corinthians 5:1-2**), until judgment day, and un-believers, (non-Christians), will go to Hades, a holding place for the lost or people going to Hell, (as in the story of Lazarus and the rich man in **Luke 16:19-31**), to wait for their final judgment on judgment day when they all will be thrown into Hell together at the same time (**Revelation 20:11-15**).   After Jesus died on the Cross, (during the three days before He showed Himself to the disciples), He led Abraham and the others in paradise to Heaven and left the un-believers, (sinners), in Hades to wait for their final judgment on judgment day (**Ephesians 4:8-9**).   So, as soon as you die, you will be standing before Jesus Christ the Son of God to be judged by Him, we all will be judged by Jesus because just as He told us in **John 14:6**; No one comes to the Father except through me.   If you have accepted Jesus Christ as your Lord and Savior and became a Christian before you died, then He will allow you to pass into Heaven, but if you are not a Christian, then **Jesus will say to you I never knew you (Matthew 7:21-23)**, and then you will be sent to Hades to wait for

44

the final judgment of Hell.   Billions of people are on their way to Hell and don't even know it, and they are going to receive a rude awaking when they die and stand before the Lord Jesus Christ, (**The Messiah**), and hear Him say, (**but I never knew you, now depart from me you who practice lawlessness**), because they are listening to men/women who contradict the teachings in the Bible and not to Almighty God. Almighty God Himself told the disciples, (when Jesus was transfigured on the mountain), that "This is My Beloved Son, in whom I am well pleased, **Hear Him**", meaning we should listen to Jesus Christ and no one else (**Matthew 17:2-5, Mark 9:2-8 and Luke 9:29-34**).   You will never go wrong if you just follow the Word of God and do what God tells you to do.   Just remember we are trying to get to God in Heaven and live forever with Him, He is not trying to come down here on earth and live with us, so we must follow His rules and directions if we want to go to Heaven and live with Him.   And please remember that everyone will be resurrected from the grave, either to go to Heaven to be with God and Christ or Hell to be with satan and his demons (**John 5:29**).

God Has Reconciled the World Back to Himself

God has made a way for men/women to have a close and personal relationship with Him again, (like Adam and Eve did before they sinned in the Garden of Eden), and He has also made away for us to come and live with Him forever in Heaven, and that way is through the death of Jesus Christ His Only Begotten Son (**2 Corinthians 5:19, Colossians 1:20**).   Our salvation cost God a lot, He had to allow His Only Son to die on the Cross and shed His Holy Blood to save us, the payment for all of our sins, (sins Jesus never committed **2Corinthians 5:21**), but He had to do it to save us from Hell, because our sins had separated us from God (**Isaiah 59:2**), and there is no way that we could have a relationship with God without our sins being forgiven, because "**GOD is Holy** and **His eyes are Pure**", and He cannot look on sin or wickedness without judging it, and then doing something about it (**Habakkuk 1:13**). Jesus's death on the Cross for the forgiveness of our sins is the reason why God did not kill us for the very first sin that we committed against

45

Him, as He should have, instead God extended His Grace and Mercy towards us to give us another chance, and this is another reason why people should be thanking God for sending Jesus Christ because God's Grace and Mercy Only comes through the Cross of Jesus Christ (**John 1:17**).   God allows the blood of Jesus Christ to cover our sins so that He does not judge us immediately for all of the sins that we have committed against Him (**Romans 3:21-26 and Ephesians 2:7-8**), and because Jesus died on the Cross for our sins, they are now covered by His Holy blood and are nailed to the Cross as forgiven (**Colossians 2:13-15**).   Now God can overlook them and work in our lives to lead us to Him for salvation and eternal life, this is called Grace and mercy.   And Grace and Mercy only comes through the Cross of Jesus Christ, there is no other way that we can receive it (**Romans 5:2**).   People do not realize that the only reason that they are still alive today is because of the Blood of Jesus Christ, His Blood is protecting them from the judgment of God, (**Yes that same Jesus they refuse to believe in**), is the only reason that they are alive today.   Honestly speaking, we all should have died a long time ago, (the moment we committed our first sin against God), because as I mentioned above, "**GOD is HOLY**", and He does not tolerate sin of any kind.   So, whatever you are doing right now just stop what you are doing and thank Jesus for dying and protecting you from God's judgment of your sins, and then thank God for giving you another chance to get it right because He did not have to.   God gave us **1 John 1:9** so that we can come to Him in prayer and ask for the forgiveness of our sins and not be punished for them, this is His way of giving us another chance.   But if we do not ask Him for the forgiveness of our daily sins, then He is going punish us for these sins (**Hebrews 12:3-11**).   God loves us so we should thank and Glorify Him every day for sending Jesus Christ into this world to die for our sins so that He can offer us a second chance, because as I said earlier some people do not get a second chance when they sin against God, some of the people in the Bible, as well as some people living today, died after committing their first sin against Him (**1 Corinthians 10:1-11**).

Why Jesus Christ is the Only Way to God and Heaven

John 14:6 Jesus said to him, **"I am the way,** the truth, and the life.   **No one comes to the Father except through Me".**

When God made Mary, the mother of Jesus pregnant, He shielded Jesus from the sin in her body by the Holy Spirit coming upon her, and the Power of God overshadowing her, this also protected her from the Holiness of Jesus which would have killed her if any part of her sinful body would have touched Him (**Luke 1:34-35**).   Jesus is God and He is Holy, so He had to be born in a Holy environment, this is why the Holy Spirit had to come upon and overshadow Mary.   This is also how He was born Holy and sinless, and this is why God will not accept any other sacrifice for sin except the Holy Blood of Jesus Christ.   Jesus's Blood is Perfect, Holy and Pure, (meaning never tainted by sin), and this is why God will only accept His Blood for the sacrifice for sin because the sacrifice for sin must be perfect and Holy like God, and there was no one on earth like that, so He had to send down His Only Begotten Son Jesus Christ to save mankind from sin, and because Jesus is God, so His Blood is Holy like God His Father (**Hebrews 2:17 and 7:26**).   We have been Justified by His blood and reconciled to God through the Cross of Jesus Christ our Lord and Savior (**Romans 5:8-11, Hebrews 10:10 and 12-14**).   If you belong to a church that does not teach on the Blood of Jesus or the Cross of Christ, then you need to leave that church and find a church that does because you can only be saved through what Jesus did on the Cross, His death, burial and resurrection, and you can only be justified by the shedding of His Holy Blood for your sins (**Romans 5:9-11**).   I will say it again if the Church you are attending is not teaching salvation through the Blood and Cross of Jesus Christ, (then you need to leave that Church), because you cannot be saved unless you hear the message of the Cross of Jesus Christ, (The Gospel), as it is taught in the Bible.   When you believe and confess these truths, and ask Jesus to come into your life and be your Lord and Savior, then you will be saved/

Born Again (**Romans 10:9-13**), and then you will receive the Holy Spirit from God (**Acts 2:38**). The Holy Spirit will be **Sealed inside** of you (**Ephesians 1:13**) making you a son/daughter of All Mighty **God** (**2 Corinthians 1:22**) and a member of the Body of Christ His Holy Church (**1 Corinthians 12:13-14**). After salvation the Holy Spirit will begin to change you into the person God wants you to be, someone just like His Son, Jesus Christ our Lord and Savior (**Romans 8:29 and 2 Corinthians 3:18**). When you receive Jesus as your Lord and Savior, you will become a (**Born Again Christian**), a real **Christian**. If you are not a Born Again Christian, **then you are not a Christian at all**. I do not care what someone else has told you or how much you go to church or how much you read the Bible, or how much you listen to gospel music or watch Christian T.V. until you ask Jesus Christ to come into your life and become your Lord and Savior, you are not Born Again, and you are not a Christian. I know you have heard some people say that it doesn't take all that, (meaning you do not have to be Born Again to be a Christian), but what they are telling you is not true, because Jesus our Lord and Savior told Nicodemus in (**John 3:3-8**), unless one is Born Again, he cannot see the Kingdom of God. So, if Jesus Christ Our Lord and Savior said you must be Born Again to become a member of His family and to be **a Christian**, then you must be Born Again to be a Christian and to become a member of God's family. This includes every man/woman on earth no matter what nationality they are, everyone must be saved/Born Again to become a Christian, and to enter Heaven. For there is no difference, (meaning nationality of people black, white green or yellow); for all have sinned and fall short of the glory of God, as the Bible teaches us in (**Romans 3:9-18 and 21-26**). So, if someone is telling you that you do not have to be Born Again to be a Christian, (they are lying to you), and this is a clear sign that this person is not a Christian. Anyone that contradicts what the Word of God teaches is not a Christian, because they are calling **God and Jesus liar's**, so do not believe or even listen to them, this is a clear sign that they are not of God because the Bible teaches us in **John 3:34** that for whom God has sent speaks the Words of God, so whoever teaches something that contradicts what the Word of God teaches is not of God, they are of the devil/satan. Please, listen and understand what I am trying to explain to you, Jesus died for the forgiveness of all of our sins (past, present and future), every single one, (sins that He did not commit), Jesus is the One that hung on that Cross and died for you and I, not the person who is telling you these lies, so if Jesus Christ said you must be Born Again to enter the kingdom of God, then you must be Born Again, Jesus said it and God the Father made sure it was written down for us in the Bible, and now we must do it.   Jesus our Lord and Savior said in **Luke 11:23** that he who is not with Me is against Me, and he who does not gather with Me scatters, and this means that if someone is not teaching salvation through the Cross of Jesus Christ, then they are not of God nor Christ, they are a false teacher, and they are scattering the people and sending them in the wrong direction, they are leading people away from God and Christ and not to Them.   So, stop listening to these people and find someone who believes what the Bible teaches and talk to them or search the scriptures yourself for the answer.   Just pray and ask God to show you the truth in His Holy Word the Bible, and God will guide you by the Holy Spirit to the answers that you seek, or He will send someone to answer your questions, or you will hear the answer in a sermon because God desires to be re-united with us, and He wishes that every man/woman would be saved and that they would return to Heaven to live with Him forever (**1Timothy 2:4**).   Through the Cross of Jesus Christ, God has made a way for every man/woman to return home to Heaven, but He is not going to make us come home to live with Him, this is a choice that we must make ourselves, because He does not want anyone up there who does not want to be there with Him.   You must be willing to come to Jesus to be saved (**John 5:40, 6:40**), you must choose to be with God and Christ, you must say yes or no to Them there is no neutral position.   And if you do not listen to God and follow His instructions, then this is a clear sign that you do not want to be there in Heaven with Them.   If you are not a Born Again Christian then you can never return home to Heaven or please God (**Romans 8:7-8**), no matter what you do or how hard you try. God will only accept us through the Cross of Jesus Christ His Son, Jesus said it Himself in **John 14:6** "I am the way, the truth, and the life, and **No one comes to the Father but through Me**", that's it, no more discussion.   This means that when you die you will not be allowed to see, talk or even get anywhere near to where God is, because if Jesus does not know you, then you will not be allowed to pass into Heaven. I am writing this because you always hear people say that when they die, they are going to talk to God themselves and ask Him what they want to ask Him. I always laugh when I hear people say things like that because I realize that they do not have a clue of who God is or what they are talking about, and sometimes I want to tell them so bad that it is not going to happen that way, you are not going to talk to God because you must go through Jesus Christ to get to God the Father, and because you do not have a relationship with Him (**God the Son**), you cannot even see **God the Father** or get anywhere near Him. I always pray for these people and ask God to help them understand who He really is and to show them what they need to do to get to know Him. And Pastors please stop calling people Christians who are not Christians. I hear it all the time on Christian T.V. and radio or when I go to different Church's, the Pastor will say, "and there are Christians sitting here right now who have not accepted Jesus Christ as their Lord and Savior". Pastor's if they have not given their lives to Jesus Christ, then they are not a Christian, they are still an un-believer and not Born Again, and you pastors are confusing these un-believers because they think that they are Christians because you, (their Pastor), are calling them one (a Christian). So, they leave Church thinking everything is alright, but if something happened to them and they died right after leaving church, then they will go to Hell, so please explain to them that you must be Born Again/Saved to become a Christian, and if you have not given your life to Jesus Christ, then you are not a Christian (**Romans 10:9-13**). Let me try to make this as clear and direct to you as possible, you are not getting into Heaven unless you give your life to Jesus Christ and be Born Again/Saved. Jesus told us this in **John 14:6** when **He said that He is the way, the Truth and the life** and **No one comes to the Father but through Him.** God the Father sat on His Throne in Heaven and watched closely as mankind mocked, spat on, beat and then crucified **His Only Begotten Son Jesus Christ** on a Cross, and I am telling you now that **He is Never going to forget** what happened to His Son (**Matthew 27:27-54, Mark 15:11-38, Luke 23:13-48, John 19:1-37**). God is **Never** going to forget what happened to Jesus Christ His Only Begotten Son, He's **Never** going to let it slide and He's **Never** going to let mankind forget what they did to His Only Son, if Jesus was your son would you forget it?   And God is **Never** going to forget what His Son had to go through so that men/women can be forgiven of their sins so that they can make it into Heaven and not go to Hell.   So, if you think that God is going to overlook what happened to His Son and let you into Heaven just because you were nice to someone, or you worked in the church, or because you gave money for a cause, then you are fooling yourself because He is **Never** going to forget what happened to His Son and what He did for mankind.   So, I am going to say this again for the last time, if you do not give your life to Jesus Christ and be Born Again/Saved before you die, then you are not getting into Heaven, and you will be sent to Hell forever, it's just that simple.

God Has Freed Us from The Grip of Sin

God has freed us from the grip of sin and temptation through the Cross of Jesus Christ our Lord and Savior.   The Apostle Paul verifies this truth in **Romans** chapter **7:24-25** when he said in verse **(24)**, (O wretched man that I am! Who will deliver me from this body of death?), and in verse **(25)** he gave us the answer, (I thank God--through Jesus Christ our Lord!).   This is why I said earlier that **you must be Born Again**, and that you must believe that God is in control of everything in your life, and you must also believe that everything God has written in the Bible is True, everything, (no questions asked).   Read the book of **Romans** chapters: **5,6,7,8**, and if you understand **Romans 6:1-22**, especially **Romans 6:2,6,7,11,14,18** and **22**, then you will live like **Romans 8: 1-15**, if you do not understand **Romans 6:1-22**, then you will live like **Romans 7:15-21**.   At least 90% of all Born Again Christians are living like **Romans 7:15-21**, (For what I will to do, that I do not practice, but what I hate, that I do), and I did also before God taught me these truths.   Why are most Christians being defeated by sin and temptation, for one thing, most believers are not being taught that they can have victory over their sin, and for the believers who are being taught this message most of them do not believe that it is true.   They read it in the Bible and then they say that God does not mean it literally, that your body is dead to sin.   So, the bottom line is this, they are

51

calling God a liar because they are saying that what He has written in the Bible is not true.   And most of them say this because they look at their life and how sin has defeated them time and time again instead of praying to God and asking Him to teach them how to walk in the spirit so that they can say no to their sins, and then they will experience how their bodies will react under the Power of the Holy Spirit.   The Bible teaches us in **Numbers 23:19** and **Titus 1:2 that God does not lie**, and in **Hebrews 6:18** the Bible teaches that **it is impossible for God to lie**, so if God cannot lie, then this means that everything written in the **Bible Must Be True**.   So, you must make up your mind today either you going to believe God or you are not, it's just that simple, because if God says that your body is dead to sin through the Cross of Christ when you are filled with the Holy Spirit, then your body is now dead to sin.   What believers need to do now is to take these scriptures and read and study them, and then ask God to teach them what they mean and how to apply them in their life.   Pray to God and say Father I believe that what you have said in these scriptures are True, now please teach me how to use and apply them in my life against my sin, in Jesus name I pray Amen. For you to have victory over the sin in your life you must believe that everything that God has written in the Bible is True!

Even though we have been Born Again and filled with the Holy Spirit of God, sin itself remains inside of our bodies making it possible for you and I to sin again, and this is why God allows satan to tempt us to sin, He wants to draw out all of our sinful desires that we have inside our flesh/bodies to transform us, (Born Again Christians), into the people He wants us to be, people like Jesus Christ His Son (**Romans 8:29**). God brings these sins and temptations to the surface in our lives so that we will know what they are, and then God will teach us how to control them.   Please listen to me, believing in God and what He has written in the Bible is the only way that you are going to experience true victory over sin and temptation.   Because you cannot do it without Him, this is what we call a catch 22, (meaning you can't have one without the other), you must believe God and His Holy Word the Bible to have true victory over sin and temptation.   If you do not believe God, then you will not have victory over your sins and temptations, because satan and sin are just too powerful.   And if you try to do it without Him, then you will continue to live in defeat as you are doing now.   I am trying to make this as plain and as simple as I can, **you will not have victory over sin and temptation without God**.   But if you take Him at His Word and believe what He tells you to believe and then do what He tells you to do, then things can only get better.   What do you have to lose?   Allow God to re-new your mind with the teachings in **Romans** chapters **5, 6,7**and **8**, and watch and see how your life changes, and then you be the judge.   So, for the next 30 days read and study the book of **Romans** chapter's 5,6,7 and 8, and before you begin to read pray to God and say;

> **Father God,** I now surrender my mind, soul and spirit unto you and your **Holy Spirit**, now please allow me to see and understand what you want me to see and understand as I read your word.   Please give me ears to hear and eyes to see and wisdom to understand your word, thank you Father for helping me Amen.

You will never be the same again.   Now, if you are not a Born Again Christian, (meaning you have not accepted Jesus Christ as your Lord and Savior, and His death on the Cross for the forgiveness for your sins), then this message will not help you at all.   Because you cannot live for God without the Holy Spirit's help, and you cannot receive the Holy Spirit until you ask Jesus Christ to come into your life and save you from your sins, and then He will make you a Christian, A Born Again Christian.   The promises in the Bible are for God's children, (Born Again Christians), not non-Christians/un-believers.

We Must Un-Equally Yoke the Church of Christ (2Corthinians 6:14-16)

Because we have allowed un-believers who are not Born Again to join the Church and then be placed in positions of leadership within the Church, (Pastors, Elders, Deacons and anyone that is employed by the church), is one of the main reasons **why we do not see miraculous signs** of healings, tongues, people being raised from the dead, revival and other miraculous signs that will Prove and Display to the World the

Power of God.   Most of the Church's that people attend today are
carnal, having little or no effect on the world around it.   The message
coming from most Churches today is not the Gospel of Jesus Christ, the
messages do not convict nor confront the members of the Church about
their sins, and is not transforming the members of the Church nor the
communities that surround it.   These un-saved speakers/leaders are not
preaching the Word of God like it should be preached, because they
cannot because they are not Born Again which means they cannot hear
from God, so we end up getting a watered-down version of the Gospel
full of worldly wisdom and jokes.   The messages from these false
teachers are leading people away from God and Jesus Christ and not to
them, they are teaching people to love and go after the things of this
world, (money, houses, power and influence…etc.), and not leading
them to God and Christ so that they can develop a close and personal
relationship with Them.   There are un-saved men/women who preach
in churches all over the world, they sound like they are saved but they
are not, they have downloaded someone else's message from the
internet, and then they preach it on Sunday as if they wrote it
themselves.   These un-saved speakers have the nerve to stand in the
front of God's House with His Holy Bible sitting in front of them, and
God, Jesus Christ, the Holy Spirit and the Angels looking down at
them, and then they perpetuate a lie acting as if this message was
written by them to the people sitting in the church.   Whoever can do
this is probably not Saved/Born Again, because they show no fear or
respect for God, Jesus and the Holy Spirit in God's House the Church.
The person who wrote the message was probably Born Again, but the
person who downloaded it and used it is probably not, so when you
hear these pastors preach their message it sounds like he/she is
Saved/Born Again, but they are not, they are a false teacher and a fake
Christian, they are lying to you and performing and act to mislead their
congregations, and this is why we now must ask our leaders if they are
Born Again/Saved.   If you listen to Christian radio like I do, then you
will start to notice that some of the pastors are using the same sermons
on every subject, with no changes to the content.   Their sermons have
the same wording, they use the same jokes and examples that was used
by another pastor that might have taught on the same subject a minute

ago, this can only mean one thing, they are downloading sermons from the internet.   And I know this is true because I heard another pastor preach about it on Christian radio.   He said that he had gone to a pastor's conference and the pastors sitting at his table with him were all talking about their golf games and how they played golf every day, so he was surprised because he said it takes him all week to get his sermon together for the Sunday service, he said that he does not have a lot of free time to do anything.   So he said to himself that I am going to hang around these guys so that I can learn how they are writing their sermons so fast, he said that this information will help him be a better pastor so that he can have some free time to do other things that needed to be done, he said that he did not play golf but he could use the free time for other things.   The Pastor then said after hanging around those other pastor's all morning and talking to them, that's when he realized that all of them were downloading sermons from the internet.   He said the other pastors told him about a website for pastors only where you can pay to download any sermon you want on just about any subject, and this is why these pastors had so much free time to play golf.   He said that they told him that all that they did was to first download the sermon from the internet, and then you practice it a couple of times during the week, and then you just preach it to your church on Sunday, and that's it.   The rest of the week you can do what you want to because the sermons are written by good pastors, so you don't even have to check them out to see if they are biblically correct.   He said that he was surprised and appalled that a pastor would download sermons from the internet and preach them as if they had written them themselves, then he said but this is what the church has become in the 21st century.   Lazy pastors and false teachers are being allowed to become leaders in the house of God, and no one is saying anything about it.   Other pastors know about it, but they are too afraid to say anything about it because they will lose friends and not be invited to big events, in other words, they are cowards.   Well now you know what is going on inside of most churches in Christendom, now what are you going to do about it, this is why we must ask our leaders if they are Saved/Born Again.   Real Pastors are Saved/Born Again and are Called by God, meaning they have heard God call them and tell them that He wanted them to Preach the Gospel of Jesus Christ, and they get their sermons from Him, while on the other hand a false teacher/pastor is someone who is not saved and has not been Called by God to Preach, they became Preachers for other reasons or because someone noticed their ability to communicate, and then that person told them that they should become a Preacher. A Born Again/Saved Pastor is God's Anointed messenger that has heard God called them to preach the gospel of Jesus Christ, and He can be use by God to do His will and an un-saved pastor cannot, and this is why God is not going to use an un-saved person to display His Power through signs and wonders. These false teachers/pastors are not Saved/Born Again so they are not God's Anointed Messengers, so do not be afraid to expose them and their false teachings whenever you hear it. We must speak out against these false teachers so that people needing to get saved can hear the real Gospel of Jesus Christ as taught in the Bible. A fake Christian is someone who has been around real Christians long enough that they have learned how to act and talk like one, these are the goats and the tares that Jesus talks about in the Bible in (**Matthew 13:24-30, 25:31-46**), Judas Iscariot was a goat/tare. But I am here to let all of the fake Christians know that you are only fooling yourself because the Holy Spirit is going to let all of the real Christian's know that you are not saved when you come around them, you cannot fool Him. My message to the fake Christians and the un-saved pastors is to give your life to Jesus Christ before it is too late, because sooner or later God is going to expose you for who you really are, and then you will be embarrassed and exposed to the whole world. Just like in the Parable of the wheat/tares and the sheep/goats God is going to send His angels to separate the wheat/sheep from the goats/tares, and then the angels will throw the goats and the tares into Hell while the sheep and the wheat go to Heaven to be with God.

And then, (what makes matters even worse), is that these same un-believers are sitting side by side with Born Again Believers making decisions for the Church, which leads to all kinds of confusion among believers in the House of God because the un-saved people are trying to bring worldly teachings and music into the church, while the Born

Again Believers are trying to keep it Holy and Godly, (**Romans 16:17-18, Jude 1:16-19**). The time has come where we as Born Again Believers must ask **our leaders and everyone** employed by the church if they are **Born Again/(saved)**, if they are not, then these leaders and employees must be asked or made to step down from their leadership position until they give their life to Jesus Christ and become Born Again/Saved.   Why we must do this, because God is not going to use an un-saved person to do His work for Him, you must be Born Again. God has drawn the line in the sand, and that line is His Holy Word the Bible and the death of His Only Begotten Son Jesus Christ on a Cross to die for our sins, which transforms Born Again Believers into the children of God and place them into the Kingdom of God.   God's only Son gave His life so that all of mankind can be saved and have eternal life, and God is not going to forget what His Son did for us and what He had to go through to save us from our sins, and anyone who does not honor His Son's death by giving their life to Him for Salvation, God is not going to let them do anything for Him, because if you do not Honor the Son, then you do not Honor the Father (**John 5:23**).   In the Bible, God has told us what to do and how to do it, and He is only going to use Born Again Christians to do His Work.   Born Again Christians are people who love, honor and respect His only begotten Son Jesus Christ by giving their lives over to Him, because they believe that He died and gave His life for them, to pay the price for their sins and to save them from Hell, and they want to show their love for Him by serving Him for the rest of their life, and a un-saved person has not done this, and this is why God is not going to use them or allow the honor received by the person who He uses to do something for Him to be given to an un-saved person, that honor should only be received by a Saved/Born Again Christian.   What we must realize is this, Born Again Christians are the Only people on Earth that God trusts, because we are His children and His Holy Priesthood, and because we really believe in Him and everything that He has written in the Bible.   God knows that we will do whatever He asks us to do, this is why we are here at this moment in time, and this is why He saved us, He knows that Born Again Christians will do His will and take the Gospel of Jesus Christ to ends of the world for Him.   Real Born Again Christians are here to do God's will, and then they will make sure that God receives all of the Glory for the work that was done, we are not here to get rich are to draw attention to ourselves.

Pastors must be Born Again so that the Gospel of Jesus Christ is preached with God's transforming power and effect so that the Church of Jesus Christ functions the way it should. We have all of these different denominations, some started by false teachers, thinking that their way is the right way instead of everyone looking at Jesus Christ and seeing that He is the right and only way, these schisms in the Church causes divisions and confusion among the members of the body of Christ, keeping them from working together as a team to make sure God's will is done (**1 Corinthians 3:3-7**). I am making this as clear as I possibly can to you, when you read the Bible you will see that there are No Denominations mention in it, so if you are not Born Again/Saved and filled with the Holy Spirit of God, then you are Not A Christian, and you will go to Hell when you die if you are not Saved/Born Again. Jesus Christ drew the line in the sand when He said in **John 3:3** that you **MUST BE Born Again** to see the Kingdom of God, I do not care what denomination you are a part of, (Baptist, Methodist, Catholic, Muslim, Mormon, Jehovah Witness, Buddhism…etc.,), if you are not Born Again/Saved, then you are not a Christian. And If you are not Born Again/Saved, then you should not be allowed to Preach the Gospel or be employed by the Church of Jesus Christ. Born Again Christians are God's children, we are a Holy Priesthood that God can call on to do His will/work at any moment, from praying for someone to healing someone, are leading someone to Salvation **1Peter 2:9**. Miracles from God come through the Holy Spirit of God, the Holy Spirit is performing the Miracles not the person He is using. The Apostles did not do any miracles until after the day of Pentecost when they got Saved/Born Again and filled with the Holy Spirit of God, there are two exceptions, in **Matthew 10:1 and Luke 10:9** when Jesus Christ gave them the power to cast out demons and to heal people who were sick, all of the other miracles they did were done after the day of Pentecost **Acts 2:43, 3:1-10, 8:4-8, 10:11**. He cannot use an un-believer because they do not have the Holy Spirit inside of them, the Holy Spirit is the One who will in power the believer to carry out God's will/work.   There are 2 different kingdoms that exist in the world today, the Kingdom of God and the kingdom of this world that we live in where the devil operates, both kingdoms are controlled by God using His angels and Born Again believers to carry out His will and plans.   You cannot do God's work in the world we live in unless you are Born Again/Saved, (which transforms you into His Kingdom), because satan and the lusts of this world are going to try and draw you back into this world's system, and without the power and help from the Holy Spirit, you will give in to it and return.   Satan can easily control an un-saved person in this world's kingdom, but not a Born Again Christian who is a member of God's kingdom.   Remember Power and Miraculous signs come through the Holy Spirit, and only Born Again Christians are filled with Him, and this is why God will only use them. This is also why we must stick to the teaching of the Gospel of Jesus Christ as the Bible instructs us to, and do not promote any denominations or organizations that teach that their way is the best way to God and Christ.

A Christian is a follower of Jesus Christ, we are not concerned with what denomination we are a member of, we are not conservatives, nor liberals, we are followers of Jesus Christ, we are like the Christians that you read about in the Bible.   We have given our lives to Jesus Christ and we are here to serve Him and to do God's will and work, we are here to make sure that the Gospel of Jesus Christ is being preach until the Lord returns, we don't choose sides because as for as we are concern Jesus Christ is the only way and the right way, and whoever does not agree with Him is wrong on the matter.   Born Again Believers are filled with the Holy Spirit of God and we are trying to follow God and do His will, while un-believers are not, they are still trying to please themselves and the world.   And this is why a non-believer should never be allowed to make any decisions for the house of God, these decisions are Spiritually discerned, (meaning they are Spiritually given to a Born Again Christian by God through the Holy Spirit of God, who then helps the believer to carry out God's plan), and an un-believer can never receive them and will never be able to

59

understand them because they are not Born Again, and they are not filled with the Holy Spirit of God, so they will not be able to hear nor understand Him (**1 Corinthians 2:13-16**).   This is also the difference between a Born Again Believers interpretation of Bible scripture and a un-believers interpretation.   You always hear people say that there are many different interpretations of Bible scriptures, but this is not true, you only have 2 types of Bible scripture interpretation, Holy Spirit led interpretation and worldly wisdom, (natural man), led interpretation. All Born Again Believers should have the same Bible interpretation because we are all filled with the same Holy Spirit (**1Corinthians 12:13, Ephesians 4:4-6**), and non-believers will always have a different interpretation from us because they are not filled with the Holy Spirit of God.   The Holy Spirit is the Person that teaches Born Again Believers the truths in the Bible, while un-believers are trying to interpret the Bible using their worldly wisdom.   So, when you come across someone who has a different Bible interpretation than what the scriptures are teaching, then you are probably talking to someone who is not saved/Born Again, and they are trying to interpret the Bible using the wisdom of this world.   If someone you know is teaching a different interpretation of Bible scriptures than what you teach and understand, if you are Born Again, then you should ask them where did they get their answers from, and then ask them if they are Born Again because this is the only way that two people can have a difference in the interpretation of the same Bible scriptures, one is saved and the other person is not.   Even if their interpretation is from someone else, (aka their pastor), someone is not saved, either it is their source or it is them, so ask them questions to find out how they got their answers, and then you might have to teach them the correct interpretation and then lead them to Salvation.   An un-believer can give advice to the Church, in areas not related to the direction that the Church should function, but Only Born Again Christians directed by the Holy Spirit of God should be making decisions for the Church of God and how it functions. Only Born Again Christians should be allowed to join the Church of God and Jesus Christ and not un-believers.   If a person cannot say that they have given their life to Jesus Christ and are saved or that they want to give their life to Jesus Christ right now before they join the Church, then they should not be allowed to join the Church. The Church is a body of Born Again Believers working together to fulfill Gods will, we are not a social club, we are God's fellow workers, we have ordained work to do, we get together for a reason to promote the spread of the Gospel of Jesus Christ (**1 Corinthians 3:9**). The only thing an un-believer should be allowed to do in the Church is to continue to come to Church and hear the Word of God until the Lord saves them, and then they can join the Church of Jesus Christ. Un-believers should not be expected to tithe to the Church either if they want to give then allow them to give, but make sure you explain to them that giving money has nothing to do with salvation or becoming a Christian. As the Bible teaches in **2 Corinthians 8:5** the people in Macedonia first gave themselves to the Lord, and then they gave an offering to the Church. Salvation cannot be bought or worked for it is **a gift from God** (**Ephesians 2:8**), and you need to ask God to save you. I know some of what I am saying sounds a bit rough, but you have to remember that we are dealing with life and death decisions here, people will either end up in Heaven or Hell, and we want them to make it to Heaven. We live in a world where there are thousands of different religions, every one of them having a different way to God, so we must preach the truth of salvation through Jesus Christ are many of them will not learn about the only true way to God and get saved. In some cases, there is going to be an entire generation of a family, (all in Hell together), because they believed and listened to false teachings from these false religions. The entire family, (father, mother, sons, daughters and grandkids), all lost and in Hell together---forever!! So, let's get the message out and maybe we will be able to save some of them before it's too late.

False Teachings in the Church

Because the members of the church have allowed un-saved people to become leaders and workers in the church of Jesus Christ, we now have numerous false teachings and false religions in the body of Christ. These false teachings like the word of faith, the prosperity gospel, positive profession…and many more are leading believers into a false sense of belief that nothing will go wrong in their lives, they will not get sick and that they are all going to be rich. Anyone who believes these teachings must be deceived, because all you have to do is to open your eyes and watch the news and you will see sickness and poverty all around you, including inside the church. The messages from these false teachers are leading people away from God and Jesus Christ and not to them, they are teaching people to love and go after the things of this world, (money, houses, power and influence…etc.), and not to God and Jesus so that they can develop a close and personal relationship with them. The bible teaches us not to love this world and the things in it, and not to store up treasures on earth, why, because sooner or later it's going to break down and fall apart, and then that money has been wasted on something with no real value (**Matthew 6:19-21**). The false teaching call the Prosperity Gospel is proof of this miss direction leading its members away from God and Christ to the things of this world. God has told us in His Holy Word the Bible that **No one** can serve two masters; for either he will hate one and love the other, or he will be loyal to the one and despise the other. God has told us in the Bible that **You cannot serve** God and mammon **Matthew 6:24,** and these false teachers preaching the prosperity gospel are saying that you can, so these men/women are calling God a liar. This is a clear sign that this teaching is not from God, because it contradicts with what the Word of God teaches us in **Matthew 6:24**. This means that these men/women who are preaching the prosperity gospel are lying to their church members, they are preaching something that does not agree with what the Word of God is teaching, this is why this is a false gospel. God is not going to give you something that will harm you are lead you away from Him, and there are no scriptures in the Bible that teach believers to name or claim for anything. Listen to me and let me make something very clear to you, just because you are a Christian does not mean that God has to do what you want Him to do, you can go around and make all of the positive confessions you like, but if God says No to your request, then the answer is No, you cannot make Him change His mind no matter how many times you ask Him. A lot of you Christians, (Born Again /Saved), are listening to these false teaching that tell you that you can confess something and it must happen just because you professed it in Jesus's Name. No this is not

True, God can still say no to your request, a lot of you think that just because you pray in the name of Jesus that you can tie up God's hands and now He has to give you what you have asked for, but no this is not true, your request must be a part of God's will and plan for your life, He's not following our life plan we are following His plans for our lives.   There is no positive professing for money are things in Bible scripture, just praying to God for help and guide onus to teach us how we should live to please Him, and then He said that He will give us what we need.   Think about it for a minute, if we can do positive confessing and make things happen the way we want them to happen, then don't you think that the Apostle Paul would have done it to keep himself from being beheaded, and the other Apostles also, because they all died some horrible deaths.   If positive professing is true why did the Apostles die the way they did?   Why didn't they just profess their deaths away, because if anybody really needed to do it, it would have been them, to stop their deaths from happening the way they did. These false teachings about positive confessions are not true, because like I said earlier this is not of God, and it is not in the Bible.   Our God and Father tells us to seek first the kingdom of God and all these things will be given to you because your Father knows what you need (**Matthew 6:31-34**), this is why these teachings are not of God like I said earlier they are not in the Bible.   We as Believer's in God and Christ need to preach and listen to messages that can be found in the Bible, the Holy Word of God, and not lies and false teachings made up by men/women.   Remember people who are sent by God will teach and speak the Words of God, and their words will line up with what God has written in the Bible (**John 3:34**), so don't listen to any teaching that does not line up with what the Bible teaches.   Remember if they cannot show it to you in the Bible, (and in context), then do not believe them because they are lying to you, no matter who the information is coming from, they are lying to you.   And if they change the words in a bible scripture to make it say what they want it to say, then they are still lying to you because we are not supposed to change the Word of God, (**Proverbs 30:5-6**).   God will only make things come true that He has promised us in His Holy Word the Bible, not false teachings made up by men/women that will trick Believers into giving more money to the Church so that they can steal it and get rich. The members of these so-called prosperity churches are the living proof showing that their pastor/false teacher is lying, most of them have been naming and claiming for things and money from 1 to 30 years in these churches, and they still have not received it, they are still just as broke today as they were when they began.   Their lives are the living proof that shows that these teachings are a lie, and not from God.   These false teachings teach their members to desire to be rich, and all that they have to do is to name it and claim it and God will give it to you, and this is not true because God has already told us in **James 4:3** that if you ask for money just to spend it on yourself, then He is not going to give it to you.   The only person that is rich in these churches are the pastor's, and they are rich because they are stealing God's tithes and offerings and spending it on themselves, and they also give some to other members of the church that will do what they tell them to do and ask no questions, and all of the other members of their church just suffer.   What these men/women are doing is nothing new, they are just acting like their older brother Judas Iscariot who use to steal money from Jesus's offering bag (**John 12:6**).   These false teachers/pastors are not fooling anyone, especially God, He knows exactly what they are doing and He is going to judge them when the time is right (**2Peter 1-3, 9**).   God is giving them enough time to see the error of their ways and repent and turn back to Him, but if they do not change, then He is going to do to them what my mother used to do to me when I was young and acting bad, she would say to me, I am giving you just enough rope to hang yourself, and then when I reached that point of no return and she has had enough, she would then whip me for the wrong that I had done, and the wrong that I was going to do in the future.   These teachings are not from God, and you do not have to believe me just Look for it in the Bible, show me in the Bible, (in the New Testament), where someone has given their life to Jesus Christ, and then God made them rich, just show me one scripture where this can be found.   When Jesus restored Peter in **John 21:15-17** He told him that if he loves him, then he should feed and tend to His sheep, not to lie to them and then try to rob them of everything that they have.   Stay away from these false teachings because they are scattering believers and leading them away from God and Jesus Christ, keeping them busy running after money and things instead of spending time in prayer trying to find out what God wants them to do for Him.   God has ordained work for every Born Again Believer to do while we are down here on Earth, that's why He saved us, and we will not find out what that is unless we spend time with Him in prayer.   Through prayer, God can show and tell us exactly what He wants us to do for Him, and then the Holy Spirit will help us carry out His plans.   The harm that these false teachings can cause is this, when the followers of these churches do and say exactly what their pastor has told them to do and say to get money and material things from God, and then God does not give it to them, these believers are going to be mad and disappointed with someone, and in most cases, they going to get mad and blame God, because He did not give them what they have asked for, and then they will say that God is not real or that He does not love them.   They never get mad at the pastor who told them these lies, NO, they always blame God.   This disappointment will make some of them leave the church and doubt their faith in God, some of them will never return, all because they believed a lie taught by an un-saved false teacher, someone who should have never been allowed to preach and teach these kind of messages in the Church of Jesus Christ in the first place.   So, please Born Again Believers, let's stop these false teachings now, expose them where ever you find them, Amen.

Hell is A Real Place

Hell is a real place and if you die without Jesus Christ, then God will send you there, (why), because He said that He would in the Bible. If God talks about Hell in the Bible, then this means that it already exists somewhere, we just don't know where it is and we cannot see it.   God does not talk about things that are not real, and secondly going to Heaven or Hell when you die is too serious of a subject to play around with, and He wants us to come to Heaven to live with Him and not go to Hell. This is why He made men write the Bible so that we would know what to do to get to Heaven where He is.   In **Hebrews 6:18, Numbers 23:19 and Titus 1:2** teaches us that God cannot Lie, **Hebrews 6:18** states that it is **Impossible For God To Lie**. So, If God cannot lie, then He will send you to Hell if you die without Jesus Christ because He said in the Bible that He would, (**this is a promise from God**). And because God cannot Lie this means that He never breaks His promises, so, He must keep His Word/Promise and send you to Hell. Please listen to Me, if God says that He is going to do something then He is going to do it because He does not lie, He never fails and He always keeps His word/promises. Just read the Bible and see how God has always kelp His promises to men and women when He told someone that He was going to do something He always did it every single time unless He was testing the person to see how they would react. And if God says that you are forgiven, then He really forgives you, and if He says He loves you, then He really loves you, so don't worry about Him not loving are forgiving you when you do something wrong, God is not like us He really forgives us when we ask Him too, and this is why He gave us the scripture **1John 1:9**. But on the other hand, if He says He is going to get you, then He is really going to get you. Why because He cannot lie, and He means everything that He has said in the Bible. This is why I know that God is going to do It, **He is going to send people to Hell who die without Jesus Christ**. So, I plead with you to listen to God and do what He tells you to do, because if God tells you that you are going to Hell if you die without receiving Jesus Christ as your Lord and Savior, then He is going to send you to Hell if you die without Jesus Christ. He must keep His word/promise that He has written in the Bible. Most people do not think that **Hell is a real place** but it is because God said that He made it for satan and his demons (**Matthew 25:41**), so Hell is a real place and it already exists somewhere, because God cannot Lie. So if God has already made Hell then He plans on using it, because people do not make things that they are not going to use. God loves us and He does not want us to be surprised by anything that will hurt us, and this is why He has placed examples everywhere in nature that proves His existence if you have eyes to see and want to know the truth (**Romans 1:18-21**). **Hell is a real place**, and as proof that there is a Hell, God has given us a planet that we call the Sun. Every day you look at the sun you see a living example of Hell and the Lake of Fire, you can see it, you can feel the heat that comes from it and the sun never stops shinning/burning, 24/7, 24 hours a day, 7 days a week and 365 days a year.   The Sun is so big that you can fit 1.3 million planet Earths inside of it, and if you could bring everyone who has ever lived back to life from the dead, then that population of people would fill 4 planet Earths (this is what the scientist has stated).   So, if God can make a planet like the Sun where you can fit 1.3 million planet Earths inside of it, then I am sure He can make a Hell that will fit 4, now don't you think so too.

So, please give your life to Jesus Christ today so that you will not end up in Hell.   All you have to do is just follow the instructions that God has given us in the Bible on how to become a Christian (**Romans 10:9-13**) so that you can make it to Heaven.   And when your faith is tested, (because your faith will be tested), you will be positively sure that you are a Christian, because your decision will be based on what the Bible teaches and not the opinion of men/women.   And then when someone asks you how do you know that you are really saved?, (meaning, are you a Born Again Christian), then you can say, (**Yes**), because I believe that the Bible is the true Word of God, and I trust and believe what the Bible teaches in **Romans 10:9-13** about Jesus Christ our Lord, that He died and paid the sin debt for all of my sins and I have asked Jesus to come into my life and save me from my sins and to be my Lord and savior.   When you do what the Bible tells you to do in **Romans 10:9-13** you are saved, and at that moment you will become a Born Again Christian, and then God will seal and fill you with His Holy Spirit (**Acts 2:38, 1 Corinthians 12:13-14 and Ephesians 1:13**).   If you want to become a Born Again Christian there is a Prayer in the back of this book that you can Pray to God to receive salvation and become a Christian.   Please trust in God and Jesus Christ and believe what they say and become a Christian, because they are not playing games, just as Jesus told the Jews in **John 8:24**, "if you do not believe that I am He, then you will die in your sins".   And if you die in your sins, then you will be sent to Hell for the punishment of your sins (**Revelation 20:11-15**).   As Jesus said in **John 17:17**; (that God's Word is truth), meaning that whatever God has spoken, written or has told us to do is True, and we should believe Him and follow His instruction to the last letter.   So, please listen to God and Jesus Christ and get saved before it is too late.

And remember to only believe God and the Bible, not men/women, and Please Check Everything Out before you Believe it.   Amen!

CHAPTER FIVE

The Holy Spirit: The Power from On High, The New Strong Man.

Jesus told the Apostles in **Acts 1:8**, but **you shall receive Power** when **the Holy Spirit has come upon you**; and you shall be witnesses to Me in Jerusalem, and in all Judea and Samaria, and to the end of the earth.

The Holy Spirit will give you power over Sin and temptation. Without the Holy Spirit living inside of us, we will not be able to say no to Sin and temptation when we are tempted by them, because they are too strong for men/women to control. This is why Born Again/Saved believers need to pray to God and ask Him to fill us with His Holy Spirit every day so that the Holy Spirit can give us the Power to say no to our sins. Believers also need to ask God to help us to surrender our spirits and make them sensitive to the Holy Spirit so that when He speaks to us we will know His voice and then do what He tells us to do. If Believers do not recognize His voice, then they will doubt His voice and not obey Him when He tells them to do or not to do something. The Bible teaches us that the Gifts of the Spirit are: love, joy, peace, longsuffering, kindness, goodness, faithfulness, gentleness and **Self-Control (Galatians 5:22-23)**. Self-Control meaning being able to control yourself, (mind, body and soul), in any situation you might find yourself in, especially when you are being tempted to sin. And we can only receive this type of self-control, (**real self-control**), from the Holy Spirit of God, this is the power from on high or the anointing that most preachers talk about today. They never say His name, but you will never be able to live for God without the Holy Spirit living inside of you, He is the Anointing that we receive from God (**Luke 24:49, 1 John 2:20, 27**). And He will not come inside of you until you accept Jesus's death on the Cross for the forgiveness of your sins, and then ask Him to be your Lord and Savior, at that moment, the Holy Spirit will be placed inside of you, transforming you into a Born Again Christian, and baptizing you into the family of God and the Church of Jesus Christ. This God given transformation will make your body dead to Sin, so that you can now say no to sin and temptation (**Acts 2:38**, **Romans 6:2-6, 8:9-14 and Ephesians 1:13**).

The Miracle of Salvation

The process of God sending the Holy Spirit to live inside of a sinful man or woman is part of the **miracle of salvation**. This is why Jesus's death on the Cross for the forgiveness of every Sin is so very important. Through the Cross of Christ, God forgave us for our sins, **(which cleanses us from sin)**, and now He can place the Holy Spirit inside of our bodies to live and guide us (**Colossians 2:11**). This is why I said earlier that **You must be Born Again**, or you cannot receive The Holy Spirit from God. The Holy Spirit is "**Holy**", He is the 3rd person of the God Head we call the Holy Trinity, and He cannot be placed inside of a sinful or un-holy vessel to dwell, His Holiness would kill the person, and this is why He is only given to people who are Born Again and their sins have been forgiven by God through the Cross of Jesus Christ. When you become Born Again/Saved, you will be filled with The Holy Spirit of God, and now you are a **New Creation in Christ Jesus**, (**God's Spirit living inside a human's body**) a new species of being, His own special people, there are no other creatures on earth like Born Again Christians (**1Cor 3:16-17, 6:19-20, 2Cor5:17, Ephesians 1:13-14 and 1 Peter 2:9-10**). One of the gifts that the Holy Spirit will give you is **Self-Control,** Self-Control over sin, temptations and the flesh (the flesh meaning yourself or your body).

The Holy Trinity

The Holy Spirit is the 3rd Person of the God Head we call **The Holy Trinity**, (**God the Father, Jesus the Son of God and The Holy Spirit**), some people do not believe that there is a **Holy Trinity** because it's hard for men/women to believe that God can transform Himself into 3 separate individuals, but you must remember that Jesus told us in the Bible that with man this is impossible but with **God All Things are**

Possible, and when Jesus Christ tells us that All things are possible with God, then He really means that God can do Anything, even things we can not understand (**Matthew 19:26, Mark 10:27, Luke 1:37 and Luke 18:27**).   Here are some Bible scriptures where all 3 Persons of the Holy Trinity are present together at the same time (**Matthew 3:16-17, Mark 1:9-11 and Luke 3:21-22**).   We will use **Matthew 3:16-17** for now;

(**Matthew 3:16-17**); When He had been baptized, JESUS, (**the SON of God, and He is the Second Person of the Holy Trinity**), came immediately from the water; and behold, the Heavens were opened to Him, and He saw the Spirit of God, (**the Holy Spirit of God, and He is the 3rd Person of the Holy Trinity**), descending like a dove and alighting upon Him.   And suddenly a voice came from Heaven, saying, "This Is My Beloved Son, in Whom I AM well pleased, (**GOD the Father is speaking from Heaven, Who is the First Person of the Holy Trinity**).

Jesus the Son is standing on the ground, **the Holy Spirit** is descending from Heaven and **God the Father** is speaking from Heaven, and we know it is God the Father speaking from Heaven because He said, "**This is My Beloved Son in Whom I AM Well Pleased**".   And **Here They Are**, all together in one place at the same time and in the Bible, "**The Holy Trinity**" The Father, The Son and The Holy Spirit 3 separate entities, as Jesus Christ told us in **Matthew 19:26** with God all things are Possible.   I hope this helps you believe in The Holy Trinity, and you can now use this example to show other believers that the Holy Trinity really exist.

What I am about to say to you now is very important so do not forget this, people and religions who deny the exitance of the Holy Spirit are not Christians because they are not Saved/Born Again and filled with Him, they are un-believers, no matter what they say are how they try to explain it away, they are still un-believers and not Christians.   If you are Saved/Born Again, then you are filled with the Holy Spirit of God, so there is no way that you can deny Him because you have Him living inside of you, you feel His presence (**Acts 2:38, Ephesians 1:13-14,**

2Corinthians 1:21-22).   People who deny the Holy Spirit do it because they do not have Him living inside of them, they cannot feel His presence because they are not Saved/Born Again.   Remember they deny The Holy Spirit because they do not have Him, they are not Saved/Born Again this is why they can deny Him.

The Holy Spirit the New Strongman

When the Holy Spirit is placed inside of a Born Again Believer, He becomes **the new strongman** that controls their bodies and life. Before you received the Holy Spirit from God you had to do what sin told you to do, you could not say no to it, because sin was the strongman controlling you.   From the moment that we were born as babies, (**sin that is inside our flesh, Romans 7:23**), took control of our bodies and became the strongman living inside of us, and is making us sin against God and do things that we don't want to do (**Galatians 5:17**).   Sin has been able to influence and control every man/woman on earth, and they had no power to stop sin's control over them, but now, (through the Cross of Jesus Christ), there is a New Strongman in the World, (The Holy Spirit of God).   And as the Bible teaches us in (**Matthew 12:29, Mark 3:27 and Luke 11:21-22**), **first you must bind the strong man before you can take over his house**), so when the Holy Spirit is placed inside of us, (after Salvation), He will bind up sin, (sin that is in our flesh **inside our body**), and then He will take total control of our lives and our bodies away from sin.   The Holy Spirit is now **The New Strongman** living inside of your body, giving you self-control over sin and changing you into the person that God wants you to be (**Romans 8:11 and 29**).   **1 John 4:4** also teaches us this truth, the scripture states that (You are of God, little children, and have overcome them, because **He who is inside of you** is greater than he who is in the world).   Now, Glorify God and the Lord Jesus Christ saints, because through salvation and the receiving of the Holy Spirit from God, you and your body are now **Dead to Sin**, and sin has no more control over you, you can now say no to your sins and temptations (**Romans 6:2, 6, 7, 9, 11,14,18,22, Romans 8:10 and 1 Corinthians 10:12-13**).   Every Born Again Believer in Jesus Christ has been set free from the total control of sin and satan by the filling of the

Holy Spirit of God.   Brothers and Sisters listen to me, (**you are now Free**), and you don't have to sin all the time anymore when you are tempted.   The Holy Spirit is here to help us say no to our sins and temptations by giving us the power that we will need to say no to them when we call/pray to Him for help when we are tempted by satan to sin (**Romans 8:9-11**).   And He is also here to help us when we are weak and about to sin, **Romans 8:26** teaches us this.

Romans 8:26 Likewise the Spirit also helps us in our weaknesses.
For we do not know what to pray for as we ought, but the Spirit Himself intercedes for us with groaning's too deep for words.

Please pay attention and read **Romans 8:26** slowly, this verse is divided into two different verses that have two different meanings, the first half of the verse teaches us that the Holy Spirit will help us when we are weak, either from sin, temptation or just from life's daily problems that may come our way and make us weak, (stress, hard times, illnesses…etc.), and the second half of the verse teaches us that the Holy Spirit helps us when we pray.   Just look at **Romans 8:26** there is a period after the word weakness, (NKJV has a period, some other versions have a ;), which means that statement has stopped and the next statement is starting.   But when most people read this verse they just read right over the period and continue on to the next verse without stopping are pausing to understand and receive what the beginning of the verse is teaching.   So, they miss out on this very important promise from God, that the Holy Spirit is here to help you when you are weak, and when you are going through something.   Either weakness from sin and temptation are just problems from everyday life, just pray to God, Jesus and the Holy Spirit, they are standing near and inside of us waiting, and ready to help us when we cry out to them for help.   Most of the time God protects us from sin and satan without our asking Him for help, and He does this every day and we know nothing about it.   We have no idea of how God has to plan out our every movement in our everyday life, for example, just going to work and then making it back home safely must be carefully planned out by God.   But then there are times when God allows us to go through some troubles in our lives just to let us know that it is not me/you who are controlling our lives but it is Him. These trials will make us humble and then we will realize who is really in control, and then we bow down and Glorify His Mighty name, Amen. When we pray to The Holy Spirit for Help, He will intervene on our behalf and stop satan from tempting us to sin, and then He will give us the power and strength that we will need to say no to the arousing desires that are inside of our flesh/body for that particular sin (**Romans 8:9-11**), these desires was started by the temptation/fiery dart that satan sent to our minds (**Ephesians 6:16**). Because of **The Holy Spirits help,** we now can say no to the sinful desires that lives inside of our flesh/body and not commit the sin that is associated with it. We must always remember to ask The Holy Spirit for help when we are tempted to sin.

The Ministry of The Holy Spirit

Through the Cross of Jesus Christ, God has restored men/women back to Himself, and we are now like Adam/Eve before they sinned and were **Spiritually separated** from God in the Garden of Eden. Born Again Christians are Spiritually reconnected to God through His Holy Spirit that lives inside of them, whom they received at salvation (**Ephesians 1:13**). God has **Sealed** the Holy Spirit inside of every Born Again Christian through the Cross of Jesus Christ which guarantees our salvation and His ownership of us (**2 Corinthians 1:22, 5:5 and Ephesians 1:14, 4:30**). For a Born Again Christian to lose his/her salvation, (**the Holy Spirit must be removed from the believer's body**), and there is not a single scripture nowhere in the Bible that teaches on the removal of the Holy Spirit from a believer's body, therefore **you cannot lose your salvation.** I already know what you are going to say, what about **Hebrews 6:4-6**, do these scriptures not teach that you can lose your salvation? No, they do not, just read the scriptures, verse (**6**) reads if they fall away, to renew them again to **repentance,** (**repentance**), the word in that verse is **repentance,** not **salvation.** The word salvation is not written anywhere in that verse, these scriptures are talking about someone who was Born Again and experienced and understood everything about the Christian life, and what

God was offering His followers.   But because of their love for the world and the things in it, they returned back to the world for what it has to offer them, and this is why in **2Timothy 4:10** Demas deserted the Apostle Paul.   So, as you can see in these scriptures the person did not lose their Salvation when they walked away from God, but their lives will be un-fruitful, sorrowful and have no direction until they return back to Him.   I hope this clears up **Hebrews 6:4-6** for you, because this scripture used to bother me also until I prayed to God and asked Him to help me understand what it meant, and the first thing that God brought to my attention was that the word salvation was nowhere in those verses, for some reason or another men and women are confusing salvation with repentance to help them make their case for loss of salvation.   And don't take my word for it, because Jesus Christ Himself has promised us **Eternal Security** in **John 10:27-30** and in **1 John 5:9-13,** so please pick up your Bible and read these scriptures.   You don't have to believe me, but please believe God and the Bible.   Born Again/Saved Christian Please listen to me, **You cannot lose your Salvation**, "**Please Just STOP**" and think about it for a minute, giving your life to Jesus Christ is the most important thing that a person will do during their lifetime, the Bible is full of teachings that reflect on the coming salvation through Jesus Christ Our Lord.   Now because salvation is so very important to God and Christ don't you think that if we could lose our salvation somehow that this would also be very important to Them?   If we could lose our salvation the Lord would have told us, and He would have written a whole book in the Bible explaining how a Born Again Believer could lose his/her salvation, and because He did not write about the loss of our salvation means we cannot lose it.   But I know that some of you need to hear the forever word, (meaning you are saved forever), and here it is in **Hebrews 7:25**; Therefore, He is able also **to save forever/uttermost,** (NASB/NKJV Bibles versions), **those who draw near to God through Him**, that's it **eternal security**, you cannot lose your salvation, so stop worrying about it.

You can be a Born Again Christian and Not Speak in Tongues

The Holy Spirit is the Person of the Trinity that gives out the Gifts of the Spirit to all Born Again Christians, this means that whatever Gift of the Spirit that you have the Holy Spirit gave it to you.   The Holy Spirit only give Gifts of the Spirit to Born Again Christians and not to non-Christians, here are some of the Bible scriptures that teach us what Gifts of the Spirit are, and how they operate in the Church, these are the Gifts that the Holy Spirit will only give to Born Again Christian's (**Mark 16:17, Acts 2:1-11, 1Corthians 12:1-11, 1Corthians chapter 14**). The Gift of Tongues is one of the Gifts of the Spirit that the Holy Spirit gives to Born Again Believers, and He gives this gift to whomever He chooses to give it to (**1Corthians 12:11**).   This means that you can be a Born Again Christian and not speak in tongues, only the Christians given this Gift by the Holy Spirit of God speak in Tongues.

1Corthians 12:11 But one in the same Spirit works all these things, **distributing to each one individually as He wills.**

I am writing this because there are some false teachings out there in the world that teach that if you do not speak in tongues, then you are not Saved/Born Again, and this is not true.   I am also writing this message because there are millions of Born Again Believers who are stressed out and doubt their Salvation all because someone has told them this lie, and I did also until God taught me the truth about Tongues in the scriptures above.   I have been Saved/Born Again for over 30 years and I have never spoken in tongues.   In my case when I was a new Christian, I was at Church one Sunday morning and during the worship service people started to speak in tongues, it seemed like everyone was speaking in tongues but me, so I started asking myself why don't I speak in tongues, if I am really saved then I should be speaking in Tongues to, and then I started to wonder if I was really Saved/Born Again.   So when I got home from Church I started to pray to God, and I was asking Him to give me the Gift of Tongues, an hour later I was stretched out laying on the floor of my bedroom still praying for Tongues, and while I was laying there the Holy Spirit spoke to me and said "Don't I Speak to You", and I said yes Lord, and then He said "Then why do you need to speak in Tongues?".   And at that moment The Holy Spirit sent to my mind all of the scriptures that taught about Tongues, and I spent the rest of the night reading those scriptures as He guided me through each and every one of them.   It was about 2 o'clock in the morning before I went to bed that night, and I prayed to God and thanked Him for teaching me the truth, and I promised Him that if I never speak in Tongues that I will never doubt my Salvation again.   Because that night God came to me where I was and gave to me the answers that I needed, that night I received something better than Tongues, I heard from the Holy Spirit of God Himself, and He taught me what I needed to know about Tongues. And to confirm to me that I had heard from Him, God had set it up where that starting the very next day which was Monday, and for that entire week, all of the Christian pastors that I listen to on the radio were all doing a detailed teaching on Tongues, and they all used the very same Bible scriptures that the Holy Spirit had given to me that Sunday night. I stopped stressing out and I stop doubting my Salvation because God had taught me what I needed to know, and you should do the same if you do not speak in Tongues, every Christian does not have this Gift from God, because the Holy Spirit gives it to whomever He chooses to give it to.   Now this does not mean that He will never give it to me are you one day, it all depends on the situation that we might find ourselves in, if we need to speak in Tongues to Glorify God around some un-believers to lead them to Christ, then He might give it to us, but it is still all up to Him, He makes these decisions not us.   I hope this helps you understand the teaching of the Gift of Tongues as it is taught in the Bible, may God bless you all, Amen.

The Holy Spirit is our Teacher

Before He died on the Cross for our sins Jesus said He would send us a Helper, the Comforter (**the Holy Spirit**), and that He would not leave us alone down here as orphans (**John 14:15-18**).   When Jesus returned to Heaven, God the Father gave us the Holy Spirit to guide us through life, and to teach us all truth about God, the Bible and the world that we live in (**John 14:26**).   The Holy Spirit is our **comforter, counselor and teacher** who is sent by God to dwell inside of us so that we can become the people that God wants us to be and perform the Good works that God has prepared for us to do while we are down here on earth.   The Holy Spirit is our teacher, and the Bible is the True Word of God told to men by Almighty God Himself.   God the Holy Spirit is the only person that can teach the Bible to men/women and then give us the ability to understand it, and this is why Jesus would say to the people around Him that if they had ears to hear and eyes to see, then they would understand what He was trying to teach them (**Matthew 13:9-16**).   The Holy Spirit of God will give you ears to hear and eyes to see, and this is why the Bible teaches us in **1Corinthians 2:11-14** that the Things of God are Spiritually Discerned, meaning you must be Born Again/Saved and filled with the Holy Spirit of God to fully understand the Bible, the natural man/woman, (meaning a un-saved/not born again man/woman), will never be able to understand the Bible with their human mind/knowledge.   Born Again/Saved Believers are supposed to be trying to develop a close and personal relationship with the Holy Spirit so He can teach and guide us in our everyday lives, but most Christians ignore Him.   When they Pray and Fast they call out to God the Father in Heaven and ignore God the Holy Spirit who is living inside of them, they seem to forget that He is God also, and this is why Jesus Christ said in **John 14:15-18**; that I am leaving and the Father will send you the Helper, Jesus was letting us know that He was leaving Earth and going back home to Heaven and that the Holy Spirit will be in charge of planet Earth now, so whatever God wants us to have will be given to us through the Holy Spirit of God.   While believers are praying to God the Father the Holy Spirit is setting inside of them saying Hey I am right here so just ask me whatever you want to ask me, this same thing happened to Jesus when He was here on earth when the disciples of John the Baptist asked Jesus why His disciples do not fast, I am sure Jesus was saying to Himself because I am standing right here, so just ask me whatever you want to ask me (**Matthew 9:14-15, Mark 2:18-20**).   But in reality, they ignored Him and prayed and fasted to God the Father because they did not believe that He was who He said He was the Son of God.   And this

78

is why on the mountain of configuration God told Peter, James and John to listen to Jesus Christ His Son (**Matthew 17:5, Mark 9:7, Luke 9:35**), and when we pray and fast to God the Father today He will tell us the same thing, He would say to all Born Again/Saved believers that they need to listen to the Holy Spirit of God who lives inside of you, that's why I sent Him to you.   We are supposed to Pray to God the Father in the name of Jesus Christ, (remember They All are One), but when God answers our prayers the Holy Spirit of God will be the Person speaking to us and carrying out God's plan and will for our lives, allowing are not allowing the things that we have prayed for to be done, also remember that God has a Chain of Command in place that He followers, God the Father, Jesus Christ the Son and the Holy Spirit, and He is not going to let us break His Chain of Command and try to bypass A Person of the Holy Trinity just to get Him to give us something that we want or for us to hear Him speak to us, No this is considered as disrespectful behavior toward the Holy Trinity.   Remember we must always do things God's way if we want to hear from Him or to have Him show up in the problems of life that we sometimes find ourselves in, whether good or bad.   To hear from God you must pray to Him in the name of Jesus Christ and then God will tell the Holy Spirit what to do concerning your prayers, either to allow or disallow what you have asked for, and sometimes He will even tell Him to speak to you, and then you will hear His Voice.   Yes, God still speaks to men/women the Bible itself, (Old and New Testaments), is living proof of that, Every Book of the Bible was written by a Man who God spoke to and then God told him what to write.

Born Again Believers are to listen to and get their directions from the Holy Spirit of God and no one else, not men/women nor angels, especially those who's teachings contradict the teachings in the Bible. What can an angel tell you that the Holy Spirit of God does not already know, and more important you don't know who you are really talking to when you try to talk to angels, most people who say they are talking to an angel are really talking to demons and they don't even know it. Jesus said that God will send us the Holy Spirit who will guide us into all truth and tell us of things to come, so we are supposed to listen to Him

79

and not angels (**John 16:13-15**). Always remember that there is **No New Relations from God**, believe only what is written in the Bible. If anyone tells you that they have a new revelation from God and they cannot show it to you in the Bible, then they are lying to you because in **1Corinthians 4:6** God teaches us to **not to think beyond what is written**. God has written down for us inside of His Holy Word the Bible, everything that He wants us to know about life and godliness (**2Peter 1:2-4**). So, stay away from teachings and people that tell you to seek out and talk to angels, **that angel you are talking to is a demon,** and that demon is controlling the person who is giving you this information. The Bible calls this type of demon a **familiar spirit Leviticus 19:31**, they can tell you things from your past but they cannot tell the future, because only God knows what is going to happen in the future. God has commanded us in the Bible not to seek out and talk to spirits, mediums, witches, psychics…etc., and here are the scriptures that you need to read **Deuteronomy 18:10-13, Leviticus 19:31, 20:6, 20:27, 1 Chronicles 10:13, Isaiah 8:19 and 1 Timothy 4:1-2**. Once again, (test every spirit and teaching, look for it in the Bible), there are no scriptures in the Bible that teaches us to talk to or seek out angels for advice. If you are a Born Again Christian, then what can an angel tell you that the Holy Spirit of God does not already know about, so please just pray to God and listen to the Holy Spirit for your guidance and information from God. God has set it up this way for a reason, He does not want us to get side tracked or led in the wrong direction by false teachings and evil spirits. As we grow in the grace and knowledge of God through the guidance and teaching of the Holy Spirit, we will be transformed into the people God wants us to be, (His one of a kind children, a Holy priesthood, His ambassadors representing Him down here on earth, people different from everything else on earth), being transformed day by day to be just like their older brother, their Lord and Savior Jesus Christ (**2 Corinthians 5:20, Colossians 3:12 and 1 Peter 2:4-10**). God placed The Holy Spirit inside of every Born Again Christian at salvation, and He transforms us, (from the inside out), to become like Jesus (**2 Corinthians 3:18**), and this is why Jesus said that you must be Born Again to become a Christian, a member of His Body the Church. True believers, (Born Again Christians), are not like everybody else, we have become the children of All Mighty God, and we are filled with the Holy Spirit of God (**1 Corinthians 6:19**, **Ephesians 1:13**), a Holy Priesthood used by God to spread the Gospel of Jesus Christ to all of the world, to save souls from Hell.   Our job is to let unbelievers (non-Christians) know that there is a God and that He has made a way for the sins of every man/woman on earth to be forgiven so that they can come and live with Him forever in Heaven.   We are not like everybody else, (un-believers), Christians have the Holy Spirit of God living inside of them, which makes them different from any other creature on earth.   The Holy Spirit changes Christians from the inside out and gives them the power to live for God and deal with the trials of life that they will face while living down here on earth, and He gives us the strength to say no to our sins and temptations, something unbelievers will never be able to do, without God.   Jesus told us that you will always be able to tell an un-believer and a fake Christian, (someone who comes to church every Sunday, but has not given their life to Jesus Christ), from a real Christian, because He said that we will know them by their fruit (**Luke 6:43-45**), you will not see any evidence of the Fruit of the Spirit (**Galatians 5:22-23**) in their life only the works of the flesh (**Galatians 5:19-21**).   So un-believers can come around us and learn how to dress like us, and they can learn how to talk like us, but they will never be able to live like us, meaning, as we grow in the knowledge of God and Jesus Christ, Born Again Christians will have evidence of the Fruit of the Holy Spirit in their lives and they **should** be able to say no to their sins most of the time.   Non-Christians cannot say no to satan and the sin in their lives because they do not have the power from the Holy Spirit to do so, so satan and sin has control over them, just as they once had control over us before we were Born Again/Saved (**Ephesians 2:1-3 and 1Peter 4:3**).   When you become a Born Again Christian God gives you the power to say no to your sins through the Holy Spirit, and you can only receive these gifts from the Holy Spirit, and He only gives them to Born Again Christians the children of God, not to un-believers.   For Born Again/Saved believers to live for God and do the works that God wants us to do, then we must have a close relationship with the Holy Spirit of God, He is the One who will tell, teach and then give us the power to do what God wants us to do, so do not be afraid to talk and pray to Him, He loves us just like the Father loves us because He is God.

Born Again Christians Cannot Be Demon Possessed

Because the Holy Spirit of God is now the New Strongman living inside of the Born Again Christian's body, **they cannot be demon possessed**. For a Born Again Christian to be demon possessed the demon must enter the believer's body and kick the Holy Spirit out or bind Him somehow to keep Him under control, and there is no demon alive that can bind and control God, Jesus or the Holy Spirit. Secondly, there are no scriptures in the Bible that teach that a Born Again Believer can be demon possessed, un-believers yes, Born Again Believer's never!! So, don't worry about being demon possessed because you have the Holy Spirit of God living inside of you and He can defeat satan and all of his demons, always remember **1John 4:4**; You are from God, little children, and have overcome them; because Greater is He who is in you than he who is in the world, Amen.

The Holy Spirit is the Only Accountability Partner We Need

You hear Christian Pastors and teachers say it all the time that you need an accountability partner, someone to talk to who can help you stay on track in your Christian life. But what they forget is that your human accountability partner can lie as good as you can. And what I don't understand is that most of them are married, so what can you tell an accountability partner that you cannot tell your wife/husband, seems like he/she should be that partner right, because they know you better than most people do. It is time for Christians to get real with themselves concerning their sin problems, (**because God already knows what we are doing**), and if we are going to have victory over our sins, then we need to know and understand what we are talking about and what to do when satan attacks. Believers need to know that when satan attacks, only God can help and deliver us from his traps. We must ask God to teach us everything that we will need to know about how to live for Him and have victory over the sin in our life.   God is the only Person that can teach us how to live for Him, and then please Him with our lives, and this is why Jesus said in **John 14:15-18, 26**, that the Father will send the Holy Spirit and He will guide us into all truth, and that we should rely on Him, **He is our counselor, our helper and teacher**.   The Holy Spirit who is inside of us, (who will be there until the day that we die **John 14:16**), desires to teach and train us to do things God's way.   All believers need to set aside some time every day and pray to Him and ask Him to teach them what to do.   I am guilty of this myself, (not setting aside some time to just pray and talk to God and the Holy Spirit), daily.   Now you see why Born Again Believers do not need a man/woman to be their accountability partners because we already have one, (**The Holy Spirit of God**), someone we cannot lie to because He knows everything. Born Again Believers should try to develop a better relationship with Him, (the Holy Spirit), through Prayer instead of trying to rely on another person who cannot really help us when satan attacks.   Because when satan decides to attack you, he is going to make sure your so call accountability partner is nowhere around, and what are you going to do then?

Pray to God and ask Him to make your heart and spirit sensitive to the Holy Spirit, so you can hear and understand Him, (clearly), when He speaks to you.   Because Father I need to know without a shadow of doubt what He is saying to me, so I can follow His instructions to the last letter so that I will not sin against you.   Amen!

We should take all of our problems and discuss them with the Holy Spirit first, and then follow His instructions, and if you want to talk to a man/woman about the matter after that, then go right ahead, because you have already discussed the matter with the most important person first.   Then when satan shows up to tempt you, you will know who to go to for help first, you just stand and pray to the Holy Spirit. No fighting, or trying to out whit the devil with scriptures, just pray and talk to the Holy Spirit and turn the fight over to Him, (this is called submitting to God), He is the only One that can make the devil flee from you and I (**James 4:7**). We are only to resist satan in the faith that we have in God and His Holy Word the Bible and stand on what Jesus Christ has done for us on the Cross because we all suffer a like re-guarding temptation (**1Peter 5:9**). Living for God is not easy because satan is our enemy and he wants us to fail, but when God teaches you how to say no to your sins, living for Him will be the best thing that you will ever do. Don't worry about satan because most of the time we are hidden inside of God through Christ Jesus, so satan cannot find us (**Colossians 3:3, 2 Thessalonians 3:3**), but when God does allow us to be tested He only allows us to be tested with what we can bear (**1 Corinthians 10:12-13**), and then we must be on our guard to satan and his tricks.

Please read Romans chapters 5,6,7,8, over and over again and ask God to help you understand and believe what these scriptures are teaching. Read and study these scriptures until they re-new your mind and become a part of your belief system, and remember, **if God said it, then it is True**. These scriptures will teach you the truth of your freedom from the power of sin and temptation. You must believe what they teach, and then apply what they teach to your everyday life if you want to have victory over your sins and temptations. And remember, if God said you are free, and sin will not have victory over you, then you are free (**Romans 6:11-14, Romans 8:10-13**). Jesus Christ our Lord said in (**John 8:31-32**), and you shall know the truth, and the truth shall make you free. And in (**John 8:36**), Jesus said, if the Son makes you free, you shall be free indeed. This is why I told you earlier that **you must believe** that God is in control of everything, and that the Bible is the True Word of God, and that everything that God has written in Bible is **True,** (No questions asked). Now, **you will sin again**, this is just a fact of life, as I stated in the first chapter there is no one living on earth that does not sin, I still sin and you will to (**1 John 1:8, Galatians 5:17** and **James 3:2**). And King Solomon said it also in **1Kings 8:46**; there is no one who does not sin. Circumstances will occur that will catch you off guard and this will lead you into sin again, either from temptations, trials of life or your own evil desires. Being a Christian does not mean that we do not commit sin, but we as Christians should not be sinning more than the un-believer's do, we should be able to say no to our sins most of the time through the power that we can receive from the Holy Spirit of God.   When a non-Christian looks at our lives they should see something different about the way we act and live.   Satan is not going to leave us alone to have a peaceful life because we are Born Again Christians, the Children of God, (the God he hates), and because we are doing God's work down here on earth, so no, he is not going to leave us alone unless God tells him to.   Satan is going to set traps to tempt us to sin every chance he gets, he is going to use the desires of this world to try and trick us to sin against God our Father (**1 John 2:16**), this is the warfare between the Spirit and the flesh/body that the Apostle Paul speaks of in **Romans 7:15-23** and **Galatians 5:17**.   But, remember that when temptation does occur, you can now say no to it through Power from the Holy Spirit of God and you do not have to give in to it any longer, because you are now **Free and Dead to sin, because you are Born Again/Saved**.   If you want to become a Christian, then there is a Prayer in the back of this book that you can pray to God and ask Him to save you, because everything written in this book applies to Christians, (Born Again Christians), and if you are not a Christian, then none of what you have read will work for you.   The promises God has written in the Bible are for His children, (Born Again Christians), not to un-believers.   And remember to only believe God and the Bible, not men/women, and Please Check Everything Out before you Believe it. Amen!

CHAPTER SIX

How Do We Allow the Holy Spirit
to Control the Sin In Our Lives

What shall we say then? Shall we continue in sin that grace may abound? Certainly not! How shall we who **Died to sin** live any longer in it (**Romans 6:1-2**).

But if you **walk by the Spirit**, then you will not fulfill the lusts of the flesh (**Galatians 5:16**).

When we became Born Again Christians, God placed the Holy Spirit inside our bodies (**Acts 2:38**), and at that moment the Holy Spirit took total control of our lives and bodies away from sin, the sin that dwells in our flesh. We sin when we act out the evil desires that dwell inside our flesh/bodies. God sent Jesus Christ to earth in the likeness of sinful flesh, (He became a man), to deal with the sin problem that dwells inside of every human being (**Romans 7:17, 23 and 8:3-4**). Because the sin that is inside of our flesh is controlling us, we cannot live for God as we should, so at the Cross, Jesus Christ condemned sin in the flesh, (meaning **Jesus judged and now controls the sin inside our bodies** through the Holy Spirit given to us by God when we became Born Again). Born Again Believers, (Christians), can now control the sin inside of their flesh/bodies and prevent it from acting out and committing sins that dishonor God and also stop it from doing harm to others (**Romans 8:3-5**). As the Bible teaches us in **Matthew 12:29, Mark 3:27**, and **Luke 11:21-22; first you must bind the strong man** before you can take over his house, (so when the Holy Spirit is placed inside of our bodies after salvation), He will **bind up** sin inside of our flesh/body, and then He will take total control of our body away from sin. This transformation will make our flesh/body **Dead to sin** (**Romans 8:9-11**), and give us the ability to say no to sin and temptation. Even though the Holy Spirit has bound up sin in our flesh, the evil desires and bad habits that sin has produced in our lives will still affect our mind and bodies causing us to continue to sin, even after salvation.   This is why we now have a daily battle between the mind of Christ we received at salvation, and sin that dwells in our flesh/bodies **(Romans 7:23, 1Cor 2:16 and Galatians 5:17)**.   Most Christians do not know this because we are not taught these truths in church, so after we are Born Again, we still continue to commit the same sins we committed before salvation, and then we wonder if we were really Born Again/saved because we see no real outward change in our lives.   But in the book of Romans you will find these truths being taught in chapters 6, 7 and 8.   These chapters teach us that we are dead to sin, (after salvation), and that sin should not have control over us anymore.   When we received Jesus Christ as our Lord and Savior, we were Baptized into Him, (His death, burial and resurrection), and He gave us the Holy Spirit to help us deal with the sin that is in our lives and flesh/body **(Romans 6:2-6)**.   Through Power that we receive from the Holy Spirit of God, we can now say no to sin and temptation.   The old man has been crucified by the Cross of Jesus Christ, and we now should put on the new man and walk according to the Spirit **(Romans 6:6, 8:11-15)**.   And you do this by first believing what the Word of God teaches in Romans: 6, 7 and 8, and then you Pray to the Holy Spirit and ask Him for help when you are tempted to sin. Please read these chapters over and over again until you fully understand what they are teaching, and then you must believe in your heart that what they teach is true.   Pray and ask God to help you understand what these scriptures are trying to teach you so you can have victory over your sins and temptations, and He will help you understand and give you victory **through the Holy Spirit**, because the Holy Spirit is here to guide us and to teach us all truth, and to help us when we are weak **(John 16:13, Romans 8:26)**.   And remember that the transformation from the sinful life you once lived into the life that God wants you to live will take some time, you will not stop sinning overnight.   After salvation some of your sins will be easier to let go of than others, because God will remove the desire for that sin from your mind and flesh giving you full repentance from that sin.   And you have probably heard of someone who was hook on drugs or alcohol, and then they gave their life to Jesus Christ and they stop committing those sins that same day. The same thing will happen to you, some of your sins you will stop doing right after salvation, but some

of your other sins may take some time for you to stop doing them.   I
don't know why it happens this way but remember that everything is
done according to God's plan and not ours.   I am telling you this
because as soon as you tell people that you are now a Christian, they are
going to judge you as soon as you make your first mistake, (Christians as
well as non-Christians).   They are going to judge you and say
Christians don't suppose to do things like that, but you just tell them that
you are saved and God is still working on you in that area of your life,
and then move on.   Don't be discouraged are depressed because
everyone changes differently, it just depends on how God has planned it
out.   This is why the Bible teaches us that we must work out our own
salvation with fear and trembling through God and Christ, and not the
salvation of others (**Philippians 2:12-13**).   And always remember that
God is with you no matter what you are going through, and He is there to
help you stop sinning if you really want to stop.   All you have to do is
just pray to God and ask Him to help you when you are tempted to sin,
and He will.

There Will Be A Battle to Control You

There is going to be a battle fought inside your body between your
mind, (now controlled by the Holy Spirit), and sin that dwells inside your
flesh for the control of your mind and body as taught in **Romans 7:23-24**
and **Galatians 5:17**.   Even though you are now saved, (meaning you
are now a Born Again Christian), sin and satan will still want to control
you, and because we live in a sinful world that tempts us every day with
the lust of the flesh, the lust of the eyes and the pride of life (**1 John
2:16**), (controlled by sin and satan), we will be tempted to sin by them
until the day we die.   So, the best thing for Born Again Believers to do
is to learn how to deal with sin and temptation God's way, and the first
step in the process of handling sin God's way, will be the renewing of
your mind with the Word of God, and the second step in the process,
(which is the most important), is for the believer to be **fully convinced**
that God is in total control of everything in our lives and that we can do
nothing without Him.   Everything that happens to everyone that lives
on planet earth is controlled by God, (whether Good or Bad), He allows

things to happen to us according to His Will and plan not ours (**Acts 17:25-28**).   People need to understand that He owns us and we don't own Him, and because He made us, He can do whatever He desires to do with us, we are the clay, and God is the potter.   God saved us from Hell because He loves us and our salvation cost Him a lot, we were bought at a price, (the Blood and Body of Jesus Christ His Only Begotten Son) (**1 Corinthians 6:15, 17-20**).   God is in control and He owns everything and everybody on planet earth, some people don't like that, but there is nothing that they can do about it because it is the truth (**Psalm 24:1**). Born Again Believers are just blessed that we have a Good and Loving God as our father, who has saved us from Hell and has given us eternal life through the Cross of Jesus Christ.   On the other hand, for non-believers, (people who do not believe in God and Jesus Christ), their god is satan the devil, and most of them don't even know it, and he only comes to steal, to kill and to destroy and they will end up in Hell with him if they do not give their life to Jesus Christ and get Saved/Born Again before they die (**John 10:10**).   This is the battle that we will be fighting all of our lives until the day that we die, and if you do not have God and Jesus on your side then you will not win.

Satan Cannot Make A Born Again Believer Sin

When you read the book of Romans chapter's 6, 7 and 8 you will notice in these chapters that satan is not mention at all, (not even one time), this is because the battle is between the sin that is in our flesh/body, and the mind of Christ we received at Salvation (**1Cor 2:16 and Galatians 5:16-18**).   Satan, (the devil), cannot make, touch or do anything to a Born Again Christian without God's permission.   Always remember that Jesus has already defeated and disarmed satan at the Cross over 2000 years ago, and He made a public spectacle of him and his demons (**Colossians 2:15**), so he can only send you thoughts of temptation he cannot make you do anything through the flesh/body anymore.   So, when a Born Again Christian sins now, they have made the decision to give into the temptation that satan has presented to their minds, and then they allow their bodies to act out that temptation by committing the sin that's associated with it.   We cannot blame

89

everything on the devil anymore, we now must look in the mirror at ourselves and see our self for who we really are as taught in **James 1:21-25**, we are hearers of the Word of God and not doers.   We as believers must now ask God to teach us how to become doers of His Word so we can stop being a saint controlled by sin as explained in **Romans 7:15-21**. As soon as you realize the condition that you are in, (meaning that you are being controlled by sin), you then should go to God and asked Him to help you with your sin problem and to teach you how to say no to your sin and temptations so that you can live for Him and do His will.   Go to Him, God wants to help you, He is waiting on you.

Gift's Received by Those Who Believe in Christ

Jesus's death on the Cross gave believers in Him a place in the kingdom of God and made them children of God (**Galatians 3:26**). Believers in Jesus Christ have been grafted into God's kingdom and they have been changed on the inside, (through salvation), to become new creations in the world they live in, and their lives should be an outward demonstration of that change.   In their new position, (given to them by salvation through the Cross of Jesus Christ), Born Again Believers receive certain gifts to help them have victory over their sins so they can live for God as they should.   Born Again Believers have:

1. **Romans 6:1-2** died to sin.
2. **Romans 6:6-7** they are no longer slaves to sin because their old self was crucified with Jesus on the Cross.
3. **Galatians 5:24-25** their evil passions and desires were crucified in their flesh.
4. **Colossians 3:3** they are hidden in God through Jesus Christ.
5. **Romans 6:4-5** and they now walk in newness of life through the Holy Spirit of God.
6. **Hebrews 10:22, 9:14 and 1Peter 3:21** our evil conscience has been taken away, and we now have a good and clean conscience with God.
7. **Romans 8:9-11** and **1 John 4:4** They are filled with the Holy Spirit of God, who gives them the Power of God inside of them, and

the Presence of God with them where ever they go.

So, when sin and temptations come now, we do not have to be afraid anymore, because God the Holy Spirit, (who is inside of us), will be with us forever and wherever we go (**John 14:16**), and because He who is inside of us is greater than he who is in the world, we can now say no to our sins and temptations (**1 John 4:4**).   And God the Father has promised us in **Hebrews 13:5-6** that He will never leave us nor forsake us, and Jesus Himself said in **John 14:15-18** that He is always with us, He is inside of us, and that I will not leave you as orphans; (**I will come to you**).   God our Father, Jesus Christ our Lord and Savior and The Holy Spirit, (our councilor and teacher), will always be there for us when we need Them, so don't worry just pray/call to them for help when you are tempted to sin, Amen.

We Must Believe that God Can Do What He said He Can DO

In **Romans 8:28** God promises us that all things will work together for the good to those who love God and are called for His purpose.   These scriptures are not mere words written in a book, these are **Promises** from Almighty God Himself to His children, (Born Again Believers), He will do every single thing He has promised us that He will do, God will never let us down because nothing is **Impossible** for God (**Mark 10:27**).   We as Born Again Believers must now walk by the faith that we have in God and His Holy Word the Bible and not by sight, the things that we see all around us (**2 Corinthians 5:7**).   And for a Born Again Believer to walk by faith and not by sight, he/she must be **fully convinced** that God is in control of everything in their lives and that everything written in His Holy Word the Bible is True.   This is the only way that you will be able to do it, you must truly believe that God is who He says that He Is and that He can make all of His promises in the Bible come true, and you also must believe that He can make them come true for you.   To walk by faith and not by sight and to have victory over the sins and temptations in your life, you now must look at your sins and temptations and believe that, (because of salvation and being filled with the Holy Spirit of God),

1. your body is now dead to them and,
2. you can say no to them through Power from the Holy Spirit.

It is put up or shut up time now for the Born Again Believer. Either we believe God and what He teaches us in His Holy Word the Bible or we do not. It is just that simple, either God is telling the truth or He is lying. This is why I said earlier that you must make up **your own mind** and believe in **your own heart**, and be **fully convinced** that everything that God has written in the Bible is True. We now must walk by the faith we say we have in God and His Holy Word the Bible and not by our past failures or our present condition in life because God can change everything in our lives and the things around us in a blink of the eye. Do not worry about what other people think, you must make up **your own mind** and decide in **your own heart** if you are going to believe God or not. This is exactly what Jesus was telling the Apostle Peter in **John 21:21-22**, Jesus told Peter not to worry about what He wanted the Apostle John to do, Jesus said to the Apostle Peter **"You follow Me"**. Because when we die and stand before God and Jesus Christ, they are not going to compare our lives to any other believer's lives, we will be judged on whether we followed the instructions God gave us to follow. Our faith in God must be like that of Abraham's as mention in **Romans 4:20-25**, we must be **fully convinced** that God can perform what He promises. To have victory over the sin in your life you must be **fully convinced** that **nothing is impossible for God**, and I mean nothing **(Matthew 19:26, Mark 10:27, Luke 18:27)**. As Christians we spend a lot of time looking back at our past sins and our present condition too much, we need to focus on God and His Word and let God take care of the rest of the things in our lives. When you begin to focus your life on God and the things He wants, you will notice that everything else in your life will begin to fall into place, and then you will experience God's peace in your life. And His peace will always be with you no matter what you are going through in your life.

Christians Must Take Sin Serious

To live for God and enjoy His Peace in our lives we as Born Again Believers cannot live and act like the un-believers that we hang out with (**Ephesians 4:17-24**), because we have an adversary that roams around looking for someone to devour and his name is satan (**1 Peter 5:8**). His job is to tempt and set traps for believers so that they will sin against God, the devil knows his job and he does it very well. It took me a long time to fully understand that I could not mingle with un-believers and not sin. If you hang out with sinners you will end up sinning (**1 Corinthians 15:33**). I did not take this scripture seriously, I thought I could still hang out with sinners and not fall into sin myself because I knew I was a Christian and I thought I could control myself around sin. Boy was I wrong, and a lot of the sins that I committed, I committed because I was hanging out with the wrong people, in the wrong places and doing the wrong things. And I do not blame the un-believers that I was with because they were just doing what they always did, I blame myself because I should have known better, I should have listened to the Word of God. And because of the lifestyle that I was living, I picked up a lot of sinful habits and evil desires, and those same bad habits and evil desires have turned into the sins and temptations that I battle against every day in my Christian life.

Believers must take sin seriously as God does, and not play around with it. Christians must treat sin as Jesus instructed us in **Mark 9:43-48** you must cut off all access of sin to your life, meaning you should stop doing it today and not wait until tomorrow;

- **(43) the hand**; if you are making or planning something that will cause you to sin, (a weekend getaway with a boy/girlfriend or friends that will cause you to sin, or are you planning something that will harm someone else in some kind of way... gossip, or setting a trap for someone to fell...etc.),
- **(45) the foot**; if you are going somewhere that might cause you to sin, (are you going somewhere where you know you will be

tempted to sin just by being there),

- **(47) your eyes**; if you are looking at something that might cause you to sin, (pictures, movies, websites, magazines, T.V shows…etc.)

Starting now, Today, as a Born Again Believer you must stop all sinful acts that may cause you to sin and turn your whole life over to God and Christ because the more you commit these sins the deeper they are going to draw you into the sin itself, (**by placing a strong desire for this sin inside of your mind and flesh**).   And then satan will use this desire to tempt you to sin against God.   The desire to sin that is inside your flesh will turn into the daily battle against your spirit for the control of your life as taught by the Apostle Paul in **Romans 7:15-16 and Galatians 5:17**, and then when **Desire Has Conceived**, it gives birth to sin; and sin when it is full–grown, brings forth death (**James 1:15**).   So, do not present the members of your body to be used as instruments of unrighteousness to sin, because as I said earlier, sin will place a desire for that particular sin inside of your mind and body, making it hard for you to say no to this sin when you are tempted by it (**Romans 6:19, 7:21-23**).   But present yourself and the members of your body to **God every day** to be used for His will and purpose, and read **Romans 6:12-14 and 12:1-2**.   The Desire to Sin is very strong and powerful, and we as humans cannot control or defeat it without God's help, and this is why Jesus Christ had to come down from Heaven to save us from it (**Romans 8:3-5**).   This is also why you must try to cut off all contact with sin, (to the best of your ability), and then read and study the Word of God every day with prayer, asking God for Help and deliverance from your sins. When you read the Bible, and pray to God for help, you are opening the door that draws you closer to Him, and as the Apostle James teaches us in **James 4:8**; if you draw near to God, then He will draw near to you. And being close to God is where you really need to be right now because satan and sin are going to try and lead you back into your old sinful lifestyle again, satan and sin are not going to let you go that easy.   This is why Born Again Believers need to read and study the Bible daily, and they also need to hear the Word of God being preached either in church or over some other kind of information medium daily.   Because if you want to have victory over your sins and temptations, then you need to come before God and be in His Holy Word daily, and not just when you get yourself in some kind of trouble.   The Devil knows the sins that we like, and he also knows how to tempt us so that we will commit these sins, (the sin that so easily ensnares us **Hebrews 12:1**), and he is going to make sure our sins and desires cross our path every chance he gets.   But if you believe God and what He teaches us in the Bible, that you have been delivered from your sins at salvation, then you will not be easily defeated by satan when he comes to tempt you again.

Until you are ready to take God seriously and stop sinning, you will never have victory over your sins and temptations, or the peace that comes from God in your life.   We must ask God to search our hearts and to show us the reason why we are drawn to the sins we commit, (because there is a reason why we are drawn to our particular sins), and then we must ask Him to help us to repent and turn away from these sins and to remove the desire that we have inside of our bodies for these sins.   As the Apostle James teaches us in **James 1:14**, (each person is tempted when he or she is drawn away by **their own desires,** and then enticed).   Satan can only tempt/entice a believer, but sin that is in our flesh and our own desires for this sin will lead us to act on the temptation and commit the sin.   But, the Holy Spirit, (who is placed inside of us at salvation), will give us the power to say no to sin, satan and our desires if we pray to Him for help when we are tempted to sin (**Romans 6:12, 14, 8:9-14 and 8:26**).

Pray to The Holy Spirit When You are Tempted to Sin

All temptations begin and end in your mind before you ever act them out, this is why satan will always send you a thought, (**A Fiery Dart**), about the temptation to begin the sin process in your mind.   A **Fiery Dart** is anything that satan can use to arouse the sin that is inside of our flesh/body, which will start the sin process from within.   A **Fiery Dart** can be a thought, a phrase, a memory of something or a picture of someone, anything that will arouse the sin that is inside our flesh/body.   So as soon as the temptation starts, (when you receive the first thought in your mind about a sinful desire), you need to pray to the Holy Spirit for help right then and not later, because He is our First line of defense against sin and temptation.   In **Romans 8:26** the Bible teaches us that the Holy Spirit Will Help us in our weaknesses.   You must pray to the Holy Spirit and ask Him to help you say no to sin and temptation, (at the moment you are being tempted), and then He will intervene on your behalf and give you the power to say no to that temptation, **this is called Submitting to God**.   When you submit to God by Praying and asking Him for Help when you are being tempted to sin, you now understand within yourself that Only He can help you say no to your sins and temptations.   Submitting to God First for help is so very important especially when we are dealing with sin and temptation because as I said earlier, they are so strong and powerful, especially the Sin that so Easily ensnares us (**Hebrews 12:1**).   This temptation, **the one that so easily ensnares us has our number**, (meaning, most of the time we commit this sin when we are tempted by it), for some reason or another we are totally drawn to this sin.   This particular sin has us totally drawn to it by connecting our human desires and emotions to it, (**our own evil desires**).   This sin feels good to the flesh because we have an emotional attachment to it through our past experiences with it, and our memories of doing it reminds us of how good it feels when we do it, and satan makes sure that while we are being tempted by it that we do not remember the guilt that we will feel after we have committed this sin against God.   And last but not least we like doing it most of the time…Strike 3 You are **Out**.   The sin that so easily ensnares us is the sin that tempts you most of the time, almost every day.   You can be driving down the road or doing something important and out of nowhere you get a thought concerning this sin.   Even while Praying to God or sitting in Church this sin will still pop up in your mind, you don't have to look for it, this sin finds you.   For some believers it is a stronghold in their life, and for others it is a thorn in the flesh to keep them humble, **this is the sin that so easily snares**.   But notice in **Hebrews 12:1** that God commands us to **lay down** the sin that so easily ensnares us, and we can only do that with help from the Holy Spirit of God.   This is why we must Pray to the Holy Spirit for help as soon as possible, (ASAP), when we feel the temptation begin or even better when satan sends us the First thought, (**The Fiery Dart**), concerning any sin to our minds.   Remember temptations will always start in the mind First, satan will send a Fiery Dart to your mind concerning the Sin to tempt you, you then must do one of two things, Pray to God for Help or fight it yourself.   Most of us try to fight it ourselves without God, and then we end up losing the battle and sinning against Him.   We lose this fight because we do not understand how sin works, so when we are tempted to sin, we think we can handle it ourselves.   What we do not realize is that satan has put together a well-planned strategy for you and I that will lead us into committing a sin.   Satan has followed, watched and studied us long enough until he now knows exactly what we like, and he also knows when, where and how to tempt us to sin, everything he does is calculated to make us sin. He wastes no time and does not let any opportunity go by without using it to tempt us to sin.

This is how sin works; (**first**) satan sends the temptation to your mind to start you thinking about the sin, and then (**step 2**) before you know it your emotions and memories from your past experiences with this particular sin starts to arouse the passions inside of your flesh/body towards this temptation, and finally (**step 3**) the desire inside of your flesh for that sin starts to draw you towards committing the actual act itself, and if you cannot stop yourself at this point, then you will commit the sin.   This is why you must Pray to the Holy Spirit for help as soon as the temptation begins because once the sin process has started it is hard to stop it by yourself, **you will need the Holy Spirits help** to stop the sin process when it has begun.   We are not able to stop it on our own, it is too strong and powerful.   When you realize this, (that you cannot handle sin by yourself), then you will be willing to do it God's way.   So now it is time to try it God's way as **James 4:7** teaches us to, you need to **Submit to God,** and then Resist the devil, and **God will make Him Flee from You.**   We as Christians must realize that satan is not afraid of us and that he has the power to kill us at any time.   But because of who we are in Christ Jesus, (children of God), he dares not touch a hair on our heads without our Father's permission.   And take notice that the devil is fleeing away from you, he's not walking or waiting around for another try, this is because you have prayed to God for help and have turned the whole situation over to Him, so He can handle it however He pleases.   When satan hears you Call/Pray to the Holy Spirit for help he flees because he now knows that the Holy Spirit is coming after him for messing with a child of God, (like a mother protecting her baby), and he knows that somebody's going to get hurt and it is not going to be the Holy Spirit, so satan flees.   So, remember to Pray/Call to the Holy Spirit for help when you are tempted to sin, and I usually pray something like this:

Dear Holy Spirit, I am being tempted to sin again, (name whatever sinful desire that you normally give into, **Hebrews 12:1** the sin that so easily ensnares you), and I know that if you do not help me right now, I am going commit this sin.   I do not want to sin against You, God the Father or the Lord Jesus Christ.   So please help me right now and give me the strength and power to say no to this temptation (**Romans 8:11**), or show me the way of escape so that I will be able to bear it and not commit this sin against God (**1 Corinthians 10:13**). Thank You Holy Spirit for helping me because I cannot do this without you.   In Jesus name I pray, Amen.

When you pray to the Holy Spirit for help you have now turned the battle over to Him, someone who can defeat satan and all his demons.   Remember you summit to God by asking the Holy Spirit for help, and then you resist the devil by standing on the promises in the Word of God by saying that these thoughts are sin, and you are saying no to them through Power from the Holy Spirit of God because they violate God's laws, (and through Salvation), Jesus Christ has made your body dead to them, and now you do not have to give in to them anymore.   And if your Bible is handy read **Romans 6:1-22** and **Romans 8:1-15**.   You should now pray to God and ask Him to make the devil flee from you, and then God will make satan flee from you, and then you will begin to feel **the desire** for that temptation **fade away**, and then the temptation will stop.   I know that sounds easy, and it is because **Nothing Is Impossible for God,** and secondly, we are just doing what He has told us to do in His Holy Word the Bible, we are following the instructions in **James 4:7-8** and **Romans 8:26**.   As I said earlier you must be **fully convinced** that God can do what He said He can do, if you have any doubts in His ability to fulfill the promises He has made to us in the Bible, then you are not going to have victory over your sins and temptations.   Because you cannot have victory over your sins without God's help, and if you do not believe in Him and His Holy Word the Bible, then satan is going to use your unbelief against you every chance he gets to keep you under his control.   Satan does not want you to know that he does not have power over you anymore, (because of Salvation), He does not want you to know that you can say no to all of your temptations, (through the Power of the Holy Spirit), and that you don't have to sin every time you are tempted (**Romans 8:11**).   You must believe God and be **fully convinced** that what He has written in the Bible is true and that He can do what He said He can do.   It is time for you to walk by the faith you say you have in God and not by sight (the things you see all around you), it's put up or shut time for me and you.   Either God is telling us the Truth or He is lying to us and I am writing this as a living witness to tell you that God is telling the truth, and if He will do it for me, (giving me victory over my sins when I do what He tells me to do), then I know that He will do it for you because God shows no favoritism regarding His children, He wants the best for all of us (**Romans 2:11**, **Galatians 2:6, Colossians 3:25**).   Now God is going to allow satan to tempt and test you to see how you respond, so don't get too discouraged when you fail and sin sometimes, being tested by temptation teaches us to run to Him first for help, and failing also teaches us to stop trying to handle it ourselves. When you begin to have victory over the sins and temptations in your life your faith in God and His Holy Word the Bible will grow more and more.   But please be careful and be on guard as the Apostle Peter instructs us to be in (**1Peter 5:8**), and watch and learn when and where satan tempts you, because as I said earlier, sin is very powerful, and even though I now know what to do when I am tempted to sin, sometimes the temptation is so strong that it catches me at the right time, and then I forget everything I know to do, and I end up committing a sin.   So now I carry around with me in my wallet a list of the promises of God pertaining to my freedom from sin, and other scriptures related to my sins so that now when I am tempted and my mind goes blank, I have the Word of God with me, (**the Sword of the Spirit, Ephesians 6:16-17**), that I can pull out and use to help me remember what to do.   And remember, (before you do anything), you need to Pray to the Holy Spirit for help first, every time you are tempted, (and I mean every time you are tempted), don't take any temptation lightly, take them all serious, because they all are, I found out the hard way, and I am trying to save you some heartache and pain.

Remember what the Word of God teaches us in **Ephesians 6:13** that we should put on the whole armor of God so that we will be able to resist in the evil day.   Notice the scripture tells us to **just stand**, (not fight), but to stand on the faith we have in what Jesus did for us at the Cross when He defeated satan and his demons and paid the price for all of your sins (**Colossians 2:13-15**), and the new position in God He gave us through salvation.   You also must believe what the Word of God teaches us in Romans 6, 7 and 8, that we are filled with the Holy Spirit of God, and He makes our bodies dead to sin.   You must believe God and be fully convinced that what He has written in the Bible is True, because this is the only way that you will be able to say no to your sins, and then walk by faith and not by sight (**2 Corinthians 5:7**).   You must not depend on anything or anyone but the Lord our God and His Holy Word the Bible, because men/women will let you down and lie.   You must depend on God alone for whatever kind of help that you will need in life, no matter what kind of situation that you might find yourself in, remember to always pray to God for help first.   Remember what I said earlier, that sometimes when I was tempted that the temptation was so strong that I forgot what to do, most of the time when that happened God stepped in and shielded me from the temptation so that I could bear it and not sin.   The other times God allowed me to fall because He was teaching me a very important lesson, (that I **must take all** Sin and temptation seriously), they are all dangerous and something that you should not play around with, (because sin will place an evil desire inside of you for that particular sin), making it hard for you to say no to it. And secondly, I needed to learn that I could not handle or control the sin and temptation in my life without God's help.   God has a very serious viewpoint towards sin and temptations, (this is why He commands us in the Bible to stay away from them), and because He knows the painful consequences and addictions that are connected to each and every one of them, and this is why He teaches us that the wages of sin is death, physical and spiritual (**Romans 6:20-23**).   When satan begins to tempt us, we must take captive every evil thought that satan sends into our mind and make it conform to the Word of God (**2Corinthians 10:5**), and then pray to the Holy Spirit and ask Him to help us say no to the temptation.   At that moment the Holy Spirit will give life to our body, (the strength to say no to the desire inside our flesh for that temptation), and then we will feel the desire inside our flesh/ body for that sin begin to fade away (**Romans 8:11**).   Continue to talk and Pray to the Holy Spirit even after the temptation has passed, this will take your mind off of the temptation and will draw you closer to God and the Holy Spirit, and They will strengthen and comfort you and give you peace.   After going through this and experiencing it for yourself how the Holy Spirit delivered you from sin, this should make it clear to you that there is no way that you can have victory over sin and temptation without God and the Holy Spirit's help.   You should also realize that God fulfilled the promise that He made to all Born Again Believers in the book of Hebrews, He was there with you when you needed Him, as He said He would be in **Hebrews 13:5** I will never leave you nor forsake you, and He also promised that the Holy Spirit will be there to help us in time of weakness (**Romans 8:26**), and He did.   This is why you must be Born Again/saved as Jesus taught us in **John 3:3,** you can only receive the Holy Spirit through salvation, and you cannot live for God without His help.

The Holy Spirit Will Give You the Power to Say No to Sin

When we are tempted to sin, the Holy Spirit will take away the desire inside of our flesh that draws us toward our particular sins, and then and only then, will we be able to say no to them.   You cannot have victory over your sin and temptations without the Holy Spirit's help.   At that moment when He removes the desire inside your body for that particular sin, you will fill the pressure from the temptation start to fade away (**Romans 8:9-14**); verse (**13**) reads, but if by the Spirit you put to death the deeds of the body, you will live. Removing the desire, that we have for a particular sin can only be done by the Holy Spirit of God, and when the desire has been **fully removed** from your body and you walk away from that particular sin, you are now **fully repented** from that sin. Repentance only comes through God and after salvation, (not before), because if you can repent of your sins before salvation, then you don't need God or the Holy Spirit's help, and Jesus would have died for nothing. This is why Jesus told the disciples in **John 15:1-8** that they could do nothing without Him, because He is the vine and we are the branches, we draw our strength through Him. And you can only receive the strength to say no to your sins from the Holy Spirit, (after salvation), coming through the Cross of Jesus Christ the Son of God. And remember what God said in **1 Corinthians 10:12-13**, that all of our temptations are common to man; but God is faithful, who will not allow us to be tempted beyond what we are able to bear (meaning; if we can bear it, then we should also be able to say no to the temptation). But, with the temptation, He will also make a way of escape, that we will be able to bear it. Praying to The Holy Spirit for help is our main way of escape, we must pray to Him for help when the temptation begins and then He will direct us in the way we should go. He will either give us the power to say no to the temptation or give us a way of escape so that we can bear it.

   1 Corinthians 10:12-13 teaches us that all temptations are common to men/women, (but Born Again Christians are not just common men/women, we are filled with the Holy Spirit of God), who will give us the strength and the power to say no to our temptations and sins. Something non-believers will never be able to do because they are not filled with the Holy Spirit of God. The more you read, study and stand on the Word of God, and then give the battle to the Holy Spirit by asking Him for help when you are tempted to sin, the more victory over sin you will have in your life. Remember, (the Holy Spirit who is inside of you), is giving you the victory over satan, the flesh and your temptations, you have no power over sin and temptation without Him. And this is why Jesus our Lord told us this in **John**

15:1-8, (this is so very important, don't miss it), verse **(5)** **for without me you can do nothing,** and in **Romans 8:11 and 26** God says that the Holy Spirit will help us in our weaknesses, and give life to our mortal bodies so we can say no to temptation, this means that we cannot say no to sin and temptation without His help.

Please try to remember to read your Bible and pray to God and ask Him to fill you with His Holy Spirit every day, because you know just as I know, that we are going to be tempted to sin sometime today, and without God and the Holy Spirit's help we will end up sinning against Him---Today! Every morning before I get out of my bed, I pray a prayer similar to what the widow said to the judge in the parable of the persistent widow in **Luke 18: 2-8**. She told the judge to get justice for her, (against her adversary), because she knew that if the judge did not help her, that her adversary would do her harm. And what God is trying to teach us in this parable is not that the widow was a nag to the judge, (even though she was), but she was honest and told the judge what she really needed, because she knew that he was the only person that could help her. Every morning before I get out of my bed, I pray a prayer similar to this:

Father God I know I am going to be tempted to sin today (name the sins you are normally tempted by), so please fill me with your Holy Spirit so when these temptations come my way today the **Holy Spirit** will give me the power to say no to them. Because if you do not help me Father, I know I will fall into sin when I am tempted by these sins today, and I do not want to sin against you, the Lord Jesus Christ nor the Holy Spirit, so please help me Father--today. I thank you Father God for helping me. In Jesus Name I Pray, Amen!

Because just like that widow in Jesus's parable I know that if God does not help me today, then I will end up in sin. The Bible teaches us that the Lord knows how to deliver the godly out of temptation, and give us victory over it (**2 Peter 2:9**). Asking God for help when we are tempted to sin is the only way that we will have true victory over it. And when I pray this prayer to God in the morning, I have given Him total control of my life for that day, so whatever happens to me must come through Him for approval, whether good or bad. If most Christians would just pray to God and tell Him what they really need, then they would see and experience Him more in their lives, but because they believe these false teachings about naming and claiming stuff that they really don't need, they never experience God for themselves.

Born Again Christians Need the Word of God Every day

You must re-new your mind daily with the Word of God and look up scriptures in the Bible, (concerning your sins), and then agree with God that whenever you break these commandments you commit a sin. You should ask God to fill you with His Holy Spirit, (**Every day**), so He can control your life and help you say no to your sins and temptations. The Holy Spirit will give you the power to say no to all of your sins and temptations when you call on Him for help (**Romans 8:9-14, 1John 4:4**). We also must use the Shield of Faith when we are tempted by sin, (by believing it, praying it and standing on it), and believing that whatever God has spoken in the Bible is True, no matter what the circumstances are, this is called being **fully convinced or Real Faith in God**. The Lord our God said in **Romans 6: 2,6,7,11,12,13,14,18** and **22** that we are now dead to sin, and that we should not use the members of our bodies to commit sin, and that sin will not have dominion over us, and now by faith we should believe what God has said in His Holy Word the Bible and stand on these truths/promises when we are tempted by satan to sin. You must always remember that you are filled with the Holy Spirit of God, (no person, thing or demon can defeat the Holy Spirit of God), and the **Holy Spirit of God** will give you the power to say no to sin and the flesh (**Romans 8:11-15**). Believing God and standing on His Word, (using the shield of faith), will put out all the fiery darts that satan will send your way (**Ephesians 6:16**). When by faith you believe God and stand on what He has said in His Holy Word the Bible, you will then be able to say no to your sins and temptations, and not give in to them every time you are tempted. Remember satan cannot force you to commit a sin, he can only tempt you to sin. All temptations sent by satan are tests, they show us how close our walk with God is when we say no to them, or how far apart from Him we are when we give in to them, either way the temptation will teach us how much we really need His help. When we are tempted by sin, we must make a choice, either to honor God by saying no to the temptation or to dishonor Him and please ourselves by saying yes to it. The Holy Spirit will give you the power to say no to every temptation that comes your way, (but you must remember to Pray to Him for help), and then He will help you overcome all of your sins and temptations, (because through salvation you are now of God), and He who is in you is greater than he who is in the world (**1 John 4:4**). You must believe this, (meaning **1John 4:4**) and you must have faith in God and believe that He is here to help you and that He is more powerful than anything or anyone in this world we live in. And if you really believe that God is all powerful, then God is for you and on your side, and who or what can really be against you or harm you without His permission (**Romans 8:31**). Again, you must re-new your mind with the Word of God daily, if you want to have victory over sin and temptation. The Word of God is our direct connection to the Holy Spirit who connects us to Jesus who connects us to God (**Ephesians 2:18**). Please read and study **Romans 6:1-22 and 8:1-17**, you must believe what is being taught in these scriptures and be **fully convinced** that what they teach is true and that these truths also apply to you. Remember if God said it then it is True, because He Cannot Lie. Please read and study these scriptures over and over again until they re-new your mind and become a part of your belief system. The more you read and study them the more they will re-new your mind and build your faith in the Word of God, and then you will be able to apply these truths to your life when satan attacks you again.

God will Give You a Desire for His Word

When God begins to teach you how to do things His way, He will first begin by renewing your mind with His Word, (**He will give you a desire in your heart for it**), you will want to hear and read it every day, and if you miss a day you will know it because you will feel empty inside without it.   Reading and listening to the Word of God every day will teach you the ways of God, (meaning how He does things), and when you learn the ways of God you will then begin to experience God in every aspect of your life, you will begin to notice His presence everywhere.   His Word will be in your heart and on your mind, and when you need a scripture the Holy Spirit will send it to your mind, the correct scripture with the answer to your question or problem.   And when our desires align themselves with the desires of God, He will then help us to see clearly what is right or wrong in any situation that we might find ourselves in, because the Holy Spirit will be there helping us, and then we will desire to do what is right and pleasing to God and not give into our desires or the desires of others.   You will be able to look at your life and some of the things that have happened to you in your life, (past and present), and you will now see how God was with you in that situation protecting and caring for you so that you could make it through safely.

      To have Victory over the sin in your life you must pray to the Holy Spirit for help every time you are tempted.   And please remember what Jesus our Lord told us in (**John 15:1-8**), that we **can do nothing without Them** (God the Father, the Lord Jesus Christ and the Holy Spirit of God).   And just as the Bible teaches us in **Romans 8:31** if **they are for you**, then who or what can really be against you!!   If you are a Born Again Christian, then God is on your side and He is here to help you.   If you really believe that **Romans 8:31 is true,** then you should be **fully convinced** of God's ability to take care of you, and then you should begin to live your life as **Hebrews 13:5-6 teaches us to.**

Romans 8:31; what shall we then say to these things?   If God is for us, who can be against us?

Hebrews 13:5-6; (**5**) let your conduct be without covetousness; be content with such things as you have.   For He Himself has said, "I will never leave you nor forsake you." (**6**) So, we may boldly say: "The Lord is my helper; I will not fear.   What can man do to me?"

106

Now Silver and Gold, Cars, Houses and Money I do not have, but what I do have I give to you: In the name of Jesus Christ of Nazareth, (The Son of the Living God), I give you the Word of God containing His Promises, take them and believe in them and **Live**! (**Acts 3:6**).   If you want to become a Christian there is a Prayer in the back of this book that you can pray to God and ask Him to save you, because everything written in this book applies to Christians (**Born Again Christians**) and if you are not a Christian then none of what you have read will work for you.   The promises God has written in the Bible are for His children, (**Born Again Believers**), not to un-believers.   And remember to only believe God and the Bible, not men/women, and Please Check Everything Out before you Believe it.   Amen!

Quick Review: When Tempted to Sin You Should;

1. Pray to the Holy Spirit for help (**Romans 8:26**),
2. Tell Him the area you are being tempted in, (He already knows but this will help you identify your sins and temptations that easily snare you) (**Hebrews 12:1**)
3. Remember that God promised us in **1Corinthians 10:13** that He will not let us be tempted by more than we can bear.   So, if we can bear it then we should be able to say no to it most of the time.
4. Remember that because we are Born Again and filled with the Holy Spirit of God our bodies are now dead to sin, so I can now say no to this temptation (**Romans 6:1-22 and 8:1-15**).
5. Ask the Holy Spirit for help and the power to say no to the temptation (**Romans 8:9-11**)
6. And then thank God for delivering you from the temptation.   Amen!

CHAPTER 7

You Are Now FREE!!

And You Shall Know the Truth, and **the Truth Shall Make You Free** (**John 8:31-32**).

If the SON Makes You Free, You Shall Be Free Indeed (**John 8:36**).

Satan and Sin Cannot Tell You What to Do Anymore!!

When our Lord and Savior Jesus Christ died on the Cross over 2000 years ago, He died once for all sin, and He defeated sin and satan forever and made it possible for All Born Again Believers to be FREE from there control (**Romans 6:10, 1 Peter 3:18**). When you became a Born Again Christian you became a NEW CREATION in Christ Jesus (**2 Corinthians 5:17**), and you are now Filled with the Holy Spirit of God (**1Corinthians 6:19-20, 2 Corinthians 1:22, Ephesians 1:13-14**), which makes your body dead to sin and it's control (**Romans 6:2, 11, 18, 22**). The infilling of the Holy Spirit of God inside of the Born Again Christians body transforms their body into the Temple of GOD (**1Corinthians 3:16-17**), making it dead to sin and giving Total control of your body over to the Holy Spirit of God. This is why you must be **Born Again/ (SAVED)** to be a Christian, because this Holy transformation **ONLY Happens at Salvation,** coming through the Cross of Jesus Christ. And because you are now a Born Again Christian, satan and sin, (**the sin that is inside your flesh**), cannot control you anymore and tell you what to do, **You are Now Free. Jesus Christ has set us free** from satan, his temptations and sin, so we must now follow Jesus's example when we are tempted by them and just say no to them. In Matthew, Mark and Luke Jesus was led into the wilderness by the Holy Spirit and tempted by satan for 40 days, we only know about the details of 3 of these temptations, and each and every time Jesus was tempted by satan He quoted scriptures and said NO to the devil's requests (**Matthew 4:1-11, Mark 1:12-13, Luke 4:1-13**). Did you get it?   When Jesus was tempted by the devil, He told him NO!   JESUS said No to satan every time He was tempted by him because satan had no power over Him, and through the quoting of scriptures Jesus informed satan that **God tells Him what to do and not him**, and because He listens to God and follows His commands, satan cannot tell Him what to do.   If you go back and study each temptation that Jesus went through you will see what satan was really trying to do, he was trying to get Jesus to do what He wanted him to do, (change rocks to bread, kneel down and worship him and then jump off the temple), all commands leading to submission to his control and leadership, and Jesus said NO to all of them.   And because we are now Born Again Believers through the Cross of Jesus Christ, we are **Now Followers of God**, and satan and sin cannot tell us what to do anymore either.   That is it Saints, Now Glorify God, because when you are tempted by satan and sin again just say NO, and then tell satan and sin that **You Cannot Tell Me What To Do Anymore!**   I now belong to God and Jesus Christ, and because I am now a Born Again Christian and filled with the Holy Spirit of God my body is now the temple of God and I am dead to the sin inside of my flesh and your temptations, **SO** satan and sin **You Cannot Tell Me What To Do Anymore, Thank You Jesus Amen!!**   Just read again the three temptations of Christ, He did not argue or fight with satan, the bottom line is this (meaning what Jesus really did), He just let satan know that he cannot tell Him what to do.   Yes, Jesus did use scriptures, but He used them to correct, inform and teach satan the rules of God, the Person whom He follows and listens to, as the Bible teaches us in **2 Timothy 3:16-17**; All scripture is **given by inspiration of God**, and is **profitable for doctrine, for reproof, for correction and for instruction** in righteousness.

Jesus did not argue with satan or carry on a long conversation with him, He just told him what he needed to know and then moved on.   So, don't get into an argument or a long conversation with the devil over scriptures, because that's what he wants you to do so he can open a door/foothold into your life so that he can get you to interact with him (**Ephesians 4:27**), and then he will find a way to tempt you to sin just like he did to Eve in the Garden of Eden **Genesis 3:1-7**.

NOW for The Last Time Born Again Christian, **YOU ARE NOW FREE**, Jesus Christ our Lord and Savior has set us Free from sin and satan (**John 8:36**).

Now you must believe for yourself that you are Free, this is the only way that you will be able to live free and tell satan and sin no when you are tempted to sin.   Read and study the scriptures in this book until you believe them in your heart, and let them re-new your mind until you become fully convinced that they are true, and then apply them to your life.   God will give you the faith that you will need to believe Him and what you read in His Holy Word the Bible (**Romans 12:3, 2 Corinthians 10:15 and Hebrews 12:2**).   Reading the Bible will re-new your mind with God's word and help you become fully convinced in Him and what the Bible teaches so that you can begin to say no to sin and temptation with the Holy Spirit's help and guide onus.   **You must do your part**, you must read and study these scriptures and God will take care of the rest.   You need to pray to God and ask Him to help you understand the scriptures that you are reading, and then the Holy Spirit will help you to understand them and show you how to apply them to your life.

Punishment and Public Shame for Sin

Hebrews 12:3-11 and Proverbs 3:11-12 The Discipline of God toward His Children (Born Again Christians).

Hebrews 12:5 and 6;
(**5**) "My son/daughter, do not despise the chastening of the LORD, nor be discouraged when you are rebuked by Him;
(**6**) For whom the LORD loves He chastens, and scourges every son/daughter whom He receives."

1 Timothy 5:20 Those, (Born Again Believers), who are sinning rebuke in the presence of all, that the rest also may fear.

God is Holy and He does not tolerate sin from no one especially His Children Born Again Christians.   He punishes Born Again Believers (Christians) as well as un-believers alike when we sin against Him by violating His rules and laws.   So, when you see a Christian's sins exposed to the whole world on T.V. and through other news mediums, this is an open rebuke by God for the sins this person **has been committing** for some time.   **God always approaches** the sinning person first concerning their sins before He punishes them or openly rebukes them.   **God allows the Holy Spirit** to convict the person of their sins so that they are aware of them, and then they can pray to God for forgiveness and then ask Him to help them to stop committing these acts of sin.   As **1 John 1:9** teaches us; that if we ask God to forgive us of our sins He will, and then He will also cleanse us of all un-righteousness, but we must first come to Him in prayer and ask Him for His forgiveness and help.   If we do not ask Him to forgive us and we continue to commit these sins, then He will punish us privately first and then openly if we do not change from the private punishment, letting everyone know what we are doing.   Remember what Jesus said to the disciples, that whatever is done in the dark will be brought into the light (**Mark 4:22, Luke 8:17**).   So please go to God and confess the sins that you are committing, (no matter how many times you have committed the same sin), always go to God for forgiveness, He will forgive you, I know because I go to Him all the time.   We serve a Loving and Caring God who is patient and long suffering toward all of us, I know because I would have given up on me a long time ago, and I am so glad that God the Father is nothing like me, He always forgives me and then punishes me when it's necessary.   Born Again Believers must understand that we are not our own anymore, (meaning that we now belong to God, mind, body soul and spirit).   He owns you now because the **Holy Spirit of God** is living inside of you, so you cannot just go around doing whatever you want to do anymore, God will not let you, because you are now Born Again/Saved and have become the child of Almighty God, so when you sin now God will punish you.   For example, when you were a child and you did wrong your earthly parents disciplined you right, so now God your Heavenly Father does the same, (and I am living proof of this so just take my word for it), for we were bought at a price and God disciplines the ones that are His.   If you can sin against God and feel no guilt nor receive any punishment from God for your sin, then you are not a child of God, you are not Born Again and you are not a Christian. And if you hear someone say that God does not punish Christians that's a clear sign, (a Red Flag), that this person is probably not a Christian, so don't listen to them stick with what the Bible teaches and tell them to read these scriptures (**Romans 12:1-2, 1Corinthians 3:16-17, 6:19-20, 2 Corinthians 6:16-18** and **Hebrews 12:5-11**).

1 Timothy 5:20 teaches us why God, rebukes Christians openly when He has to, (**1**) to expose their sin and (**2**) to bring fear among the other Christians so that they will go to God in prayer for help with their sins or suffer the same open rebuke for their un-confessed sins.   This type of rebuke also lets the un-believing world know that there is a God and He still punishes sin, even the sins of His Born Again Believers (Christians), no one gets a pass when it comes to sin, no one, especially His Children.   God must show the World that He is Real and that His rules and standards are different from the rules and standards of the world, and that they must be followed or consequences of punishment will follow.   This is the only way that some people will realize that there is a GOD and that He really exists because when they see the open rebuke against a sinful act by a Christian and the shame associated with it, they are going to ask someone why did this thing happen to that person, then we as Christians can try to explain it to them and this might lead the person to Jesus Christ for salvation. So, go to God for forgiveness and help each and every time you commit a sin, no matter how many times you have committed the same sin. As I said earlier, we serve a God of Endless Forgiveness, Compassion and Love and He is waiting to shower us with it if we just do what He tells us to do and come to Him first for help (**1 John 1:9**). **You must ask God** for the forgiveness of your sins to fully experience His love and compassion. God is watching and waiting on you to come to Him for the help that you need, just like the father did in **The Parable of the Prodigal Son/Daughter Luke 15:20**. We Thank You Father God for your forgiveness and love, Amen!

As I stated earlier you must be **Born Again/Saved** to be set free from sin and satan, everything I have written is for **Born Again Christians**, if you are not a Born Again Christian then these promises will not work for you. If you want to become a Born Again Christian, then there is **a Prayer for Salvation** in the back of this book that you can pray to God and ask Him to save you. And remember to only believe God and the Bible, not men/women, and Please Check Everything out before you believe it. Amen!

CHAPTER EIGHT

Christians Must Learn to Walk by Faith and Not by Sight.

To live for God the way we should Born Again Believers **Must Really Believe** that God is who He tells us that He is in the Bible.   God Teaches us in the Bible that He is the All Powerful Creator of Heaven and Earth, and the God of All creations, seen and un-seen, and that He controls everything seen and un-seen in All creations and there is No other God but Him.   If God tells us that this is who He is, then we as Christians must really believe that this is who He really is **(Deuteronomy 4:32-40, Isaiah 45:1-25, 40:28-29, 42:5-11, 43:10-13** and many more scriptures).   When you see Him as this kind of God your faith in Him will be strong and you will have less fear in your life of what might happen to you because you will be **fully convinced** that nothing is more powerful than God, (no man, no thing and no spirit), and that nothing can happen to you without His permission.   If you are going to really walk by faith and not by sight, then you must believe that God can really do what He has promised us in the Bible that He can do. You must be **Fully Convinced,** (meaning you must believe without a doubt), that God can make all of the promises in the Bible that He has told us to believe in **Come True**, and that He can make them come true for you.   This is why the Bible talks about the faith of Abraham so much, I always wondered what type of faith did he have and how could I attain it.   While I was reading the Bible one day the Holy Spirit made it clear to me why Abraham's faith in God was so strong, and then He also made it clear to me that I can have that same kind of faith if I just believed God.   The two main reasons why Abraham had so much faith in God were; (1) when God spoke to him, he really heard the voice of God, and (2) he witnessed for himself how God provided for him and his family and made every promise that He had promised him come true. Abraham had seen God work miracles in his life with his own eyes, and no one relayed a message from God to him, when God spoke to Abraham, Abraham actually heard the voice of God **(Genesis 26:5)**. So, Abraham knew that God was real, and this **fully convinced** him that

God could do for him what He had promised him He would do, and **Romans 4:20-22** teaches us this truth.

    Romans 4:20-24 Abraham did not waver at the promise of God through unbelief but was strengthened in faith, giving glory to God, (**21**) and being **fully convinced** that what He had promised He was also able to perform. (**22**) And therefore, it was accounted to him for righteousness. (**23**) Now it was not written for his sake alone that it was imputed to him, (**24**) but also for us. It shall be imputed to us who believe in Him who raised up Jesus our Lord from the dead.

    This means that if we are going to walk by faith and not by sight, then we must also be **fully convinced** as Abraham was that God can do what He said He can do, and we must also believe that what God has written in the Bible is **True**, and I mean everything that He has written in the Bible is **True**. **Romans 4:23-24** teaches us that God made sure these stories were written down in the Bible so that our faith in Him would be strong also, and if someone else tries to teach us something that contradicts what the Word of God teaches us, then we **must not** believe them, because our faith and belief is in God and His Holy Word the Bible and not in the words of men/women. In **2 Corinthians 10:4-6** the Bible teaches us that we must cast down all arguments and every high thing that exalts itself against the knowledge of God, this means that if we receive some information that does not agree with what the Word of God teaches, then that information is wrong, and we should not believe it or use it no matter where are who it comes from. The Word of God should always have the final say so in our lives, not the words of men/women. Our undying faith in God and His promises in the Bible will strengthen us, and then enable us to make it through the trials of this world while enjoying the peace and blessings of God.

What Is Faith in God

Real Faith in God means that when He tells you something you believe that it is true.   Whenever I hear someone ask someone else what is faith, they always say "what is it really", meaning they do not know what faith is, and because they asked that question you can tell that they have a deep desire within themselves that wants to know what it is and how to obtain it.   And the other person always quotes **Hebrews 11:1.**

Hebrews 11:1 (Now **faith is the assurance** of things hoped for, the conviction of things not seen), But then they can never explain to the person what this scripture means, so then the person who asked the question walks away looking more confused than ever.   **Faith** means that when God tells or promises you something you believe Him, and then you wait for it to come true, (**The Assurance of Things Hoped For**).   Why do you wait, because God said it, and you believe Him? Christians must be **fully convinced** that God can do all of the things for His followers that He has promised them in the Bible that He will do. True Faith in God is the difference between a double minded man/woman, (a man/woman who does not really believe that everything that God has said will come true, and is true), and a man/woman who really believes God (**James 1:6-8**), and this is also the difference between a doer of the word and a hearer of the word (**James 1:21-25**). Doers of the Word believe God and they are the ones that you see working inside and outside of the church for God, their belief has actions behind it, because they really believe God.   This is why the Bible teaches us in **Romans 4:23-24** that all of the things that happened in the Bible were written down as examples not just for Abraham's sake but for ours also, righteousness will be imputed toward us if we **believe God.** **Real Faith in God** means that you **Believe Him when He tells you something** and that you are **Fully Convinced** that **He is real** and that **everything written** in the Bible is true.   Real faith in God also means that you believe that everything that happened in the Bible actually happened the way that the Bible said that it did (**Hebrews 11:6**).   The different stories in the Bible show us how God fulfilled all of His promises to the people that believed in Him, and these true stories were written down to let us know that He will do the same for us if we just trust and believe in Him also.   We should read and study these true stories and then allow them to feed and re-new our minds with the information that they teach, resulting in more confidence in God and the Bible while developing a **fully convinced** faith in Him and His power. If you are not **fully convinced** that God can fulfill what He has promised, then you will not enjoy the Christian life very much, because you will not experience victory over the sins in your life nor victory over the trials that we all must face while living down here on earth.   If you do not believe God and what He teaches us in the Bible, then you are going to be defeated by sin and satan over and over again simply because you doubt God and His abilities.   Satan is going to use that doubt against you every time you are tempted by sin, and when you are going through trials in your life.   Now for some people, this is what is needed to make them turn and seek after God for help because their Christian life is full of fear and defeat.   Being defeated by my sins is what drove me to God for the answers to my questions on how do I stop sinning so much.   I did not want to live in the fear of being defeated by sin every time I was tempted.   Because I believed that the stories in the Bible were true, so if God did these things for the people in the Bible, then why was He not doing them for me?   I knew He could do them for me, and one day I heard a preacher say on Christian radio that either the Bible is true or God is a liar.   And then he said that he knew for himself that God was not a liar, and **now you need to make up your own mind** and find out **for yourself** if God is everything that He says that He is, or is God a liar.   And when you find out for yourself that God is real, and that God is who He says that He is, from that moment on, your life will never be the same again.   To answer this question for yourself just read your Bible daily and go to God in prayer and talk to Him about everything that is going on in your life, this is called seeking Him.   And in **Jeremiah 29:11-13** God said that if you pray to Him and seek Him with all of your heart, then He will listen to you and you will find Him. So, I am begging you to just seek after God and then believe everything that is taught in the Bible concerning Him and His promises.   When you place your faith in His hands you will begin to see Him work in your life, and then your faith in Him will begin to grow more and more until you become **fully convinced** as I am. He loves you and He will never leave you nor forsake you, this is a promise from God **(Hebrews 13:5-6)**, He will always be there for you even when you are not doing what you are supposed to be doing. As I look back over my life and see some of the times that I sinned against God, I can see how He even protected me from harm even while I was sinning, some of those times I could have been killed or I could have gotten myself in some real trouble, but He protected me and made sure I made it through unharmed and safe. God is real and He is here to help you, so please just believe in Him and do what He tells you to do. When it comes to sin and temptation, if you believe God and what He teaches in the Bible, then victory over sin is yours to have, but if you do not believe Him, then you will never have victory over the sin in your life or the peace that comes from God. Victory over sin and temptation along with the Peace that comes from God go hand in hand with the faith that we have in God and His Holy Word the Bible. Because victory over sin comes from God, and He teaches us this in His Holy Word the Bible, and when you believe this you will stop trying to fight sin your way and let God handle your sin problem His way, and then you will experience God's peace. You are probably wondering where does faith come from and how does it grow to the point where we will believe everything that God has spoken and written. Do not worry about that because everything you need will be given to you by God through the Holy Spirit, and He will also develop your faith as He leads you through the trials and temptations of life. In **Romans 12:3** the Bible teaches that God has given each person a measure of faith, and if you lack faith in any situation just ask God to help you with your lack of faith or un-belief, just like the man did in **Mark 9:21-24,** and God will supply you with the faith that you will need to make it through any situation that you might find yourself in whether good or bad, all you need to do is just ask Him for help. God will give you the measure of faith that you will need to believe in Him, but you must grow that faith by seeking Him, He will not make you believe in Him. We must be willing to seek after God if we want to develop a personal and close relationship with Him, and as we seek after God our faith in Him and His Holy Word the Bible will grow.

Lack of Faith in God

Just as Faith in God will bring us closer to God and Christ, and we will notice Them working in our life, the lack of Faith in God and Jesus Christ will make us feel as if there is a distance between us and Them, leading us to not notice Them when They are working in our life. When we became Born Again/Saved believers in God and Jesus Christ we became God's Children, God really sees us as His Children, whether we believe it or not, this is how He sees Born Again Believers. And because He recognizes us as His Children, He is determined to take care of us and protect us if we do what He tells us to do, and to punish us when we do not do what He tells us to do (**Hebrews 12:5-11**). This is why it is so very important for Christians to read the Bible and find out what God wants us to do and how to do it so that we can learn how to please Him by doing things His way. God is on our side if we believe in Him and if we are willing to trust Him with all that we have and with everything that we will need in our lives. Of course, in the beginning of our walk with God, our faith is new and wavering, because we are getting to know God, and we are trying to find out if we can really trust Him to be there for us when we need Him. But as time goes by and we begin to see how God is showing up and working things out in our life for our good, whether good or bad (**Romans 8:28**), then our faith in Him and His promises should grow stronger. God also allows some bad things to happen to His Children when they disobey and sin against Him, this is a part of His teaching and training for all Born Again Believers. We have to understand that when we disobey God and commit different sins in our lives, that we are opening doors that might allow the devil to come into our lives and set up strongholds that will trap us into some type of sin and hinder our relationship with God. This is why we must do things His way and follow His directions to the last letter, we must follow the path that God has laid out for us, not turning to the left nor to the right to try and do things our way or someone else's way (**Joshua 1:7-9**). Born Again Believers need to remember that we have an enemy, (the devil), who is just sitting and waiting for one of us to step outside of God's will by committing a sin, and then he will attack us in our sin to try to make our sinful act a stronghold in our life (**1Peter 5:8**).

There are millions of Born Again Believers that are struggling with sins today that they wish that they can say no to, and then have them removed from their lives, all because they did not take God's instructions in the Bible seriously, and they underestimated the power of the devil, temptation and sin. But thanks be to God our Father that we can be freed from our sins through Power from the Holy Spirit of God because He who is inside of us is Greater than he who is in the world, He is more powerful than the devil and all of his demons combined (**1John 4:4**).

Lack of faith in God and His abilities can also have dire consequences for the person who loses his/her faith in God, and for the people who stop trusting Him when good or bad things happen to them. There are numerous examples all over the Bible of people who lost their faith in God, are forgot about Him, when He blessed them with money and power, and then there are other people who doubted His ability to care for them when He allowed them to go through some type of loss or trial. We will use the Prophet Elijah in the Old Testament for an example, because of His fear of the threat of Jezebel to kill him, he traveled 40 days and 40 nights into the wilderness to get away from her and ended up inside of a cave (**1Kings 19:1-4**). So, God came to him and asked him **"what are you doing here"** (**1Kings 19:5-9**), and then God tried to reassure him of who He was and how Powerful He is by making 3 powerful events happen right before his eyes, God made a strong wind blow, an earthquake and a fire appear out of nowhere right before Elijah's eyes (**1Kings 19:11-12**), but Elijah was still afraid of Jezebel and dying at her hands, he had more faith in Jezebels ability to kill him than God's ability to protect and save him from her. So, God said, because you have more faith in this woman than you do in Me, you are Fired as my prophet, and then God told him to get up and go anoint Elisha as prophet in his place (**1Kings 19:16**). For some reason, whenever you hear this story being preached inside of the Church, the pastor never tells you that Elijah gets fired, they always seem to skip over that part. God still used Elijah to perform several miracles after He fired him as prophet to show him that He still loved him, and believed in him and that He had never left him. God did not stop believing in Elijah, Elijah lost his faith in God. So as you can see, God will fire and remove people from His service if they lose faith in Him and His abilities, and if they keep committing sins against Him after He has warned them through the Holy Spirit, and if they were not called by Him to Preach or serve in the first place, and for not giving Him the Glory and credit that He deserves for the success of their ministries. The same thing that happened to the men/women that God used in the old testament is still happening to men/women that God is using today, as soon as God blesses their ministries with money and fame, it always go to their heads making them think that they are somebody special because of what God has blessed them with, and then they forget about Glorifying and serving God, they start lifting up themselves so that people can glorify and serve them as if they did all of this stuff themselves, and then God has to knock them off of their pedestal and take back what He has given them to let them know that it is not about them, but that it is always about Him.   Remember to read and study your Bible so that we can learn from the mistakes that the people inside of the Bible made so that we will not make the same mistakes they made and suffer the same consequences that they did, because the God we serve today is the same God from yesterday, and He never changes **(Romans 15:4, 1Corinthians 10:11, Malachi 3:6, Hebrews13:8).**   He can lift us up and He can also bring us back down whenever He decides to do it, and there is nothing that we can do about it because He is God, **The Great I AM.**   Amen.

Why Everything Written in the Bible is TRUE.

The Bible teaches us in **Numbers 23:19** that God is not a man, that He should lie, and in **Hebrews 6:18** that it is impossible for God to Lie, and in **Titus 1:2** the Bible teaches God, who cannot lie.   These 3 scriptures in the Bible teach us that **God cannot lie, at all**.   So, if God cannot lie, then this means that everything written in the Bible must be **True,** whether you believe this or not does not matter, because this is a true statement and a key part of your Christian foundation in which you must live your life by.   You must make up your own mind concerning this fact about God and the Bible, either God is telling the truth in His Holy Word the Bible or He is lying.   You must make up your own mind, right now, today and decide whether you are going to believe and trust God or not.   Believing that God cannot lie is one of the main foundations of your Christian faith because if you believe that God can not lie, then believing in Him and then doing what He tells you to do will be easy.   You will have no problem believing and then following God with all your heart when you are **fully convinced** that whatever He tells you is true.   Because everything that God has said is true, we can now do whatever He tells us to do and not worry about making a mistake, because we know that everything will be o.k., (Why), because God has said that we could do it.   We will then follow His instruction without any doubt or worry because we know and believe that God cannot lie. Knowing that God cannot lie also makes it easy for Christians to determine if someone else is teaching false doctrines are not, because we as Christians should compare what they are teaching to what the Word of God teaches, and if what they are teaching does not line up with what the Word of God teaches, then you know that they are lying, and we should not believe them.   The Bible is God's Holy Word spoken to mankind by Him, (not by **angels talking to a man** as all of the other religions were started), **the Bible is the only book where God Himself** told the writers of the Bible what to write, and He made sure that they did not make any mistakes, because they were writing down His Words and instruction to all of mankind, teaching them what to do and what not to do, and here are some Bible scriptures where God is telling men what to write (**Exodus 32:15-16, 33:9-11, Jeremiah chapter 30, 36:1-4**…etc.. Too many Bible verses to list).   The mistake that people are making today is that they have decided to listen to men/women who have listened to someone who an angel/demon has spoken to, (information that contradicts what the Bible teaches), instead of listening to Almighty God Himself.   And this is why we have so many different religions in the world today, satan has sent out demons or gone himself to speak to men/women who he has chosen to teach a new religion that is leading people away from God and Jesus Christ so that people will not get saved and go to Heaven to live with God, no they will end up in Hell with him. So tell me, what can an angel/demon tell us that God and Jesus Christ His Son do not already know are what they have already said?   This is why God spoke to men/women Himself in the Old testament and then He sent Jesus Christ His Son to speak to men/women, (**face to face**), in the New testament. Jesus Christ came down from heaven to meet us face to face because there is always someone saying that God is not real, so when Jesus Christ was here on earth people saw Him, they touched Him and talked to Him and you can find all of this evidence concerning His life inside of non-christian history books as well as the Bible. People cannot say that God is not real anymore because they saw Him face to face in Jesus Christ His Son, and this is why the Bible teaches us in **Matthew 1:23** that they shall call His name Immanuel, which is translated, "God with us." (**John 1:14, 3:13**).

When Jesus Christ died on the Cross over 2000 years ago He did everything that was needed for men/women to serve God and then make it into Heaven after they die, this is why He said **It Is Finished** on the Cross (**John 17:4, 19:28-30**). There is nothing else for men/women to do but to do what God has told us to do inside of the Bible, we are to give our lives to Jesus Christ and be Born Again/saved (**Romans 10:9-13**), and this is why the Apostle Paul told us in **Galatians 1:6-9** that if **Anyone, (men/women are an angel)**, preaches any other gospel to you let them be accursed, we are only to believe the Bible and the Gospel of Jesus Christ. I am begging you to just listen to God and Jesus Christ and not to other religions and men/women that teach something that contradicts what is taught inside of the Bible. The instructions that God has written down for us in the Bible will teach us how to live out our lives here on Earth, and give us the directions that we will need to make it into Heaven. Remember that God cannot lie, so this is why we can believe everything that is written in the Bible because the information that is inside of the Bible is what God told men to write, not an angel. And this is also why **we cannot add to or change the Word of God** to make it say what we want it to say because the Words that are written in the Bible are from Almighty God Himself. God has commanded us in **Proverbs 30:5-6**, **Revelations 22:18-19** and **Deuteronomy 4:1-2**, to not to add to nor take away from His Holy Words in the Bible. So, if someone is trying to teach you something from the bible and you can see that they have **added in or taken out a word** from the bible scripture to make their statement be true, then now you know that they are lying to you because they have just changed the Word of God to make it say what they want it to say, so do not believe them. This person is now a liar because they have changed the Word of God, so when we go back and read it in context, we will see that it does not mean what they said that it meant, and now we will know that something is wrong, they have lied to us, and this is what **Proverbs 30:6** teaches us, that the Word of God will show us that they are lying to us because it will not agree with what they are saying. This is what all of the false religions do, so when you are talking to them make sure that you have your bible with you, (are Bible App NKJV), and make them show you in the bible, and make sure that they read it in context. God has written down for us in the Bible everything that we will need to know concerning how to live life down here on earth and how to make it to Heaven to live with Him, all we have to do is to read the Bible and do what it tells us to do. There is no new revelation from God to men/women, everything you need is in the Bible, so if someone tells you that they have a new revelation from God and it's not in the Bible, then they are lying to you so do not believe them. **1Corinthians 4:6** teaches us this, that **we are not to think beyond what is written**, (in the Bible), so don't. So, if God the Father Cannot Lie, then this means that God the Son, (Jesus Christ), cannot Lie either. Jesus Christ is the Son of God and He is God, so He has the same God nature as His Father, and this means that He Cannot Lie either, everything that Jesus has said is true and will happen just as He said it will happen. And if the Son of God says that He will die and then be **Raised Up** after 3 days and 3 nights, then this is what He will do (**Matthew 16:21, 17:22-23**). So, this means that Jesus could not have died on Friday, no the Bible teaches us that **Jesus died on Thursday the preparation day** which was **The Day Before** the sabbath (**Mark 15:42, Luke 23:54, John 19:31**). We know that He did not die on Friday because the sabbath begins on Friday evening, and the sabbath is observed from Friday evening to Saturday evening as explained in **Leviticus 23:32**. **Leviticus 23:32** is explaining how to observe the day of atonement, but the information also instructs the reader in how the sabbath was supposed to be observed by the Jews, you are to observe the day of atonement as you would a sabbath day **from evening to evening**. And if the sabbath starts on Friday evening, then **the day before Friday**

125

is Thursday as **Mark 15:42** teaches us, and this is the day that Jesus Christ died.   Another reason why we know that He did not die on Friday is because the Bible teaches us that on the very next day after Jesus's death, the Jewish religious leaders went to see Pilate about securing His tomb **Matthew 27:62,** and if He had died on Friday then these leaders would have been outside doing work on the sabbath, which is a violation of the Jewish laws of that day and time, and we know that they would not do that because it could be a death sentence for them to be caught outside on the sabbath doing something that breaks the sabbath's laws.   So, Jesus died on Thursday and rose again 3 days later on Sunday morning just as He said He would, (let me count the days for you, Thursday daytime the day He died was the first day, and Thursday night was the first night, Friday daytime was the second day and Friday night the second night, Saturday daytime was the third day and Saturday night the third night, and then He Rose on Sunday morning), Jesus does not Lie because He can't, He is God.   Amen.

Powers in Heavenly Places Control this World

True believers meaning, (Born Again Christians), as well as un-believers, (non-Christians), must realize that the world in which we live in is controlled by Spirit beings, beings whom we cannot see nor control. God and His Holy Angels and satan and his evil angels, (who God allows to do things that conform to His plan), are the powers to be that are really controlling everything that happens on planet earth (**Ephesians 6:12**).   This is why we must always pray to God for help when we have problems in our life because God already knows about everything that will ever happen to us in our lifetime, (God knew about it even before it happened to us), from the day we are born to the day that we die God knows it all, and this is why He is the only Person who can fix our problems no matter how big or small they are.   God also knows about and allows accidents to happen to us sometimes, they are also a part of His plan for our lives.   Accidents happened even when Jesus was living here on earth, He talks about one in **Luke 13:3-4** when the tower in Siloam fell down and killed 18 men.   Nothing surprises God, He knows everything that is going to happen in this world even before it happens and He already has a plan in place to fix it.   Christians must realize that when Jesus said in **John 15:4-5** that without me you can do nothing, He really means it, He is trying to tell us that we are going to need His help to live for God and do His will while we are down here on earth.   When God commands us to do or not to do something, He is giving us the crucial information that we will need to survive down here, and we as Believers need to understand that everything spoken by God is a law and a command, because when God tells us to do or not to do something He expects us to follow His commands, and if we do not follow His instructions, then consequences will follow.   When we realize that there are consequences for not following God's rules, we will then begin to take His Words more seriously and then follow them to the last letter.   Without God and the lifesaving information that He has left for us in the Bible, believers would have no chance of making it through the trials and temptations that they will face in their everyday lives.   God tells us in **1Peter 5:8** that we have an adversary seeking whom he may devour, this means that satan knows that we are here and he wants to stop us from serving God and completing our Godly mission of presenting the gospel of Jesus Christ to save those who are lost.   Do you understand that God must protect us from satan and his demons 24 hours a day, 7 days a week and 365 days a year, until the day we die, so that we can complete the good works that He has planned for us to complete (**Ephesians 2:10**)? Satan is always plotting and planning temptations and traps for believers to fall into to deter them from following and believing God.   We are surrounded by danger 24/7, by powerful demons that could harm us at any time, (so God must protect us even while we are asleep), most of it we never see or experience it because everything is controlled by God and the work is done by His angels.   But there are times when something happens to us and then we realize that only God could have saved us from the trouble that just passed us by.   So always remember that no matter what you are going through that Almighty God is there with you, and He will only allow the things that He wants to happen to you, whether good or bad.   And when you are **fully convinced** that God can handle all of the problems in your life, then and only then, will you start relying on Him and the Bible for the solutions to all of the problems in your life.   Christians must walk by faith and not by sight because we cannot see our enemy, (meaning satan and his demons), and we do not have the power to stop them from harming us without God's help (**Ephesians 6:12, 2 Thessalonians 3:3**). This is why we must believe every word that is written in the Bible, because if we do not, then we have nothing to prepare us or protect us from the events of today and tomorrow. And this is why in the Lord's Prayer Jesus tells us to pray and ask God to deliver us from the evil one, (the devil and his demons), because He knew what we would be up against as followers of Him and God (**Matthew 6:8-15, Luke 11:2-4**). So now you see that our fight is not against men and women but against satan and his demons as explained in **Ephesians 6:12,** and only God, Jesus and the Holy Spirit can defeat and control them. Amen.

The Holy Spirit is Here to Help Us

Christians cannot make it without the Holy Spirit's leading, guiding and protection through the trials and temptations of each and every day. The Bible teaches in **1John 4:4**; He who is inside of you is greater than he who is in the world. The Holy Spirit is God, without Him leading and helping us every day there is no way that we could live for God and do His will. There is just too much that we would have to overcome, and as mere men/women we just cannot do it. And this is why Jesus sent the Holy Spirit to live inside of every Born Again Believer because He knew who and what we would be up against trying to live for God down here on earth. Jesus knew that we needed to be taught and protected as we lived to accomplish God's plans for our lives. Christians need to be taught the wisdom and ways of God while being protected from satan and his demons, these are some of the responsibilities of the Holy Spirit of God. And this is why you must be Born Again and take God and His commands in the Bible seriously because without them you will not be able to make it through the trials and temptations of life. This explains why God has written so many scriptures in the Bible concerning faith in Him and His Word the Bible. We must believe that the Bible is the true Word of God and that everything written in the Bible is true. We must follow the teachings in the Bible to the last letter and do exactly what they tell us to do because they all come with consequences, either blessings or punishment (**Isaiah 1:18-20**).   The Holy Spirit is here to help us live for God as we should, and there is no way that we can live for God and accomplish what He has planned for us to do in our life without the Power of the Holy Spirit living inside of us, guiding, protecting and showing us how to do things God's way and not our way.   We will need the Holy Spirit's help until the day we die, so always remember that you are from God and have overcome them, for He Who is inside of you is Greater than he who is in the world (**1 John 4:4**), Amen.

Take All of Your Problems to God

Born Again Believers need to learn to take all of their worries and cares to God, because we are His children and He really cares for us, and also because God is the only Person that can solve our problems and make things work out for our good (**Romans 8:28, 1Peter 5:6-7**). When you are **fully convinced** that God is in total control of everything and that He really cares for you and desires the best for you, (on that day), you will then pray to God and surrender your whole life to Him. God tells us in **Jeremiah 29** the good thoughts that He really has for us.

(**Jeremiah 29:11-13**) For I know the thoughts that I think towards you, says the Lord, thoughts of peace and not of evil, to give you a future and a hope.   Then you will call upon Me and go and pray to Me, and I will listen to you.   And you will seek Me and find Me, when you search for Me with all of your heart.

But until you believe this, (**Jeremiah 29:11-13**), you are going to try and handle the sin in your life your way, and then you will never experience victory over your sins and temptations only defeat.   When you finally make up your mind and surrender your whole life to God and tell Him to do with you whatever He wishes, (on that day), you will be ready and willing to do things His way, and then He will be able to teach you what to do.   Because you will now have realized that without God's help there is no way that you can control the sin and temptations in your life. And now the desire that is inside of your heart will only want to do things that are pleasing to God, and you will then begin to stay away from people, places and things that do not (**2 Corinthians 5:9**). When you are fully convinced that God can do what He said He can do and that He is in total control of everything in your life, (meaning; nothing can happen to you without His permission), then and only then, will you be able to relax and experience victory over your sins and the peace that surpasses all understanding, which only comes from God (**Philippians 4:4-7**). No more worries, (about people, places and things), because when these truths become true to you, you will then realize that God's way is the Right Way, and the only way that we should live. And then you will say to yourself, why did I not do this sooner, and you will begin to look back over your life, (as I did), and see all of the time that you wasted in your life over the years doing things the wrong way. But don't be too hard on yourself because God knew all along what it would take to get you to the place where you are now, as I told you earlier, He is in control of Everything!

We Receive GOD's Grace and Mercy Everyday

As you study God's Word and learn to lean on Him in times of trouble, your faith will grow as you see Him intervene in your life and make events work out for your good (**Romans 8:28**). We experience the love, grace and mercy of God every time we sin against Him and do not die because God said in **Romans 6:23** that the wages of sin is death and He really means that, we were supposed to have died when we committed our first sin against God because when God tells us not to do something it's a command and most of His commands have blessings and punishments tied to them. But because of Jesus's death on the Cross for the forgiveness of our sins, He forgives us and allows us to live another day. We must always remember that God is Holy (meaning He is Pure, He is Totally Full of Goodness), God is Light and there is no darkness/evil in Him at all, (**1 John 1:5**), and He does not tolerate any type of sin, no matter how little we might think it is, all sin is unacceptable to God. So please do not take His grace and mercy for granted, because some people do not get another chance when they sin, some people lose their life when they sin against God. When God forgives us, He demonstrates His love, mercy and the long-suffering grace that He has for us in His heart, because all of us know that He is not the God of one mistake, but He is the God of many mistakes. Just remembering all of the times that we have sinned against God and then when we asked Him to forgive us and He did, this alone should increase our faith in Him.   Because He has fulfilled the promise that He teaches us in **1John 1:9** when He said if we confess our sins, He is faithful and just to forgive us our sins and to cleanse us from all un-righteousness.   Everyone should pause for a minute every week and look back at the sin in his/her life and thank God for every time He has saved us from danger or forgiven us for the sins we have committed against Him over and over again.   These memories should confirm in our mind and in our heart that God really loves and cares for us, and if this does not give you faith in Him and His Holy Word the Bible, then you need to check yourself and see if you are really a believer (meaning, have you really given your life to Christ to become a Born Again Christian).   As the Apostle Paul teaches in **2 Corinthians 13:5** we must examine ourselves to see whether we are in the faith.   Remember we are talking about the Almighty God of Heaven and earth, and if you can sin against Him and feel no guilt, then you are probably not a Christian/ Born Again, because a true believer just cannot do that, because he/she has the Holy Spirit of God living inside of them and He will convict them of all sin against God the Father (**John 16:8**).   So, it all boils down to that same old question, do you believe God or not?   Your whole life as a Christian balances on this question, the way that you answer this question will determine how you will live out your Christian life, either in victory or defeat.   Because **Real Faith** is that you really believe that everything God has said is True, and that He can do whatever He said He can do, and He can do it for you, if it's His will, That's Real Faith (**Romans 4:21**).   I have explained everything to you that you need to know about God and the Bible, (in detail, that I can think of), now the rest is up to you, the decision to believe God is yours to make.   Just think for a minute, if God is for you, then who can really be against you (**Romans 8:31**), (and if you are a Born Again Christian), then **God is for you**, so don't worry about the trials of life, (because you really cannot do anything about them anyway), God uses trials to train us to be like Jesus, so all Christians will have them.   Remember to always take all of your problems to God in prayer and let Him work them out for you.   But you must be **fully convinced** that He can really work them out for you.   God said in **Hebrews 11:6** that without faith it is impossible to please Him, and that he who comes to God must first believe that **He is**, and that God is a re-warder of those who diligently seek Him.   As Jesus told the man in **Mark 9:23-24** and His disciples in **Matthew 17:19-21**, that if you have **the Faith of a mustard seed** and believe that God is who He says that He is and that **He Can Perform** what **He Has Promised** in the Bible (**Romans 4:21**), then All things are possible for you through God and Christ.   And you demonstrate **your mustard seed of Faith in God** by going to **Him First** when things happen in your life, (whether good or bad), and informing Him about your situation.   There is nothing else that I can tell you to convince you to place all of your faith in God and His Holy Word the Bible.   You now must make up your own mind on whether you are going to believe God or not, I hope and pray you make the right decision, may God bless you, Amen.   Now may our Lord Jesus Christ Himself, and our God and Father, who has loved us and given us everlasting consolation and good hope by grace, comfort your hearts and establish you in every good word and work (**2 Thessalonians 2:16-17**).   And remember to only believe God and the Bible, not men/women, and Check Everything Out first before you Believe it.   Amen!

CHAPTER NINE

The Conclusion

The most important thing to remember from this message is that you must put God first in your life and become a Born Again Christian, and then you must believe that everything He teaches us in the Bible is **True**. To see and experience God in your life you must first believe that He is real, and be **fully convinced** that He can fulfill all of the promises He has promised us in the Bible. I know you are tired of me telling you that you must believe God without any doubt, but if you do not believe in Him and what He teaches us in the Bible, then you will not have the peace and joy that comes from a personal relationship with God. Being able to live every day without fear or worry, just the peace of mind that comes with the belief that God has everything under control is what you will receive when you are **fully convinced** that **God is who He said that He is in the Bible**, The Almighty God of Heaven and the Earth, The Alpha and The Omega (The Beginning and The End of everything that exist). And all we have to do as believers is to just believe in Him and the Bible, and then let Him handle all of the problems that will arise in our lives. We must also remember the new position in Christ that we received after we became Born Again Christians and the benefits that come with our new position. Your faith in God, Jesus and the Bible is the foundation of your Christian life, and everything else in your Christian life will grow from this foundation. Your knowledge of the Word of God, your faith in God and the personal relationship that you will develop with God, Jesus and the Holy Spirit, will all grow from this foundation. This is why the above beliefs are so very important, and they must be taught to new believers as soon as they become Born Again Christians.

To have victory over the sin in your life you must put God first, you must believe that everything written in the Bible is true, and you must be a Born Again Christian. This is the same information that I told you earlier, and I am repeating it because Most Born Again

Christians do not have victory over the sin in their lives because they do not believe that everything God has written in the Bible is True. In the Bible, God has given Born Again Believers everything that they will need to know concerning how to have victory over their sins and temptations. Victory over sin and temptation comes from power given to us by the Holy Spirit of God, (who lives inside of Born Again Believers, whom we received at salvation), and our belief in God and what He teaches us in His Holy Word the Bible. Read and study the Bible every day so that your faith in God and the Bible will grow. The Holy Spirit will use the Word of God to teach you how to live for God and how to have victory over the sin in your life. Please remember that God is in control of everything, and if He said it then it is True.

This message is not a quick fix solution to your sin problem, for some of you it will be and for some of you, it will take some time before you begin to have victory over your sins. This all depends on if you are willing to put God first in your life, and if you believe what He teaches us in His Holy Word the Bible. If you have the desire to sin less and you want to live for God the way you should, then you should pray to God and ask Him to help you understand the Bible scriptures that are being taught in this book and to help you apply these teachings to your life. And then He will begin to teach you the things you will need to know from the Bible that will give you victory over your sins. Either you believe God and what He teaches in the Bible or you do not, it is just that simple. I am trying to make this as clear to you as possible, **that you must place all** of your faith in God and His Holy Word the Bible, because everything you need to know about having victory over sin is in the Bible, and that's where I found it. So, please just believe Him and do what He tells you to do because this is how He taught me to have victory over my sins and temptations.

God teaches us in the Bible that when we were saved, we became **New Creations in Christ Jesus** and that the **Holy Spirit of God** is now living inside of us, making our bodies the temple of the living God. And now because the Holy Spirit is living inside of us, we should be able to say no to every temptation that comes our way. The Holy Spirit will give us the power to say no to our temptations if we pray to Him when we are tempted to sin, and God will not allow us to be tempted beyond what we are able to bear. But of course, we are not perfect people, and we all will sin again and give into some of our temptations, this is just a fact of life (**1 Kings 8:46, Galatians 5:17 and James 3:2**). There is only one perfect and sinless person and He is Jesus Christ our Lord. So, sooner or later we all will be caught off guard by temptation and end up committing a sin against God. But if we really believe what God has taught us in the Bible, then we should now know what to do when we are tempted to sin, and **We Now Can Say No** to most of our temptations and not sin every time we are tempted. We now know to pray to the Holy Spirit for help when we are tempted to sin because we now realize that without His intervention in our life at the moment of temptation, we will not be able to say no to the temptation and it will cause us to sin. Now, because we know we will sin again at some point in our life does not give us an excuse for not having victory over most of the sin in our lives, we still have to live for God and be His ambassadors while we are down here on earth. This means we must control the sin in our lives through power from the Holy Spirit so that when un-believers look at our lives, they will see a difference in the way we respond to trials and temptation compared to the way they do.

The more you read and study Romans chapters 5,6,7,8 and re-new your mind with the Word of God, and then pray to the Holy Spirit and allow Him to help you in time of temptation, the more victory over sin you will begin to experience in your life. I hope this message will place a desire in your heart to get to know God, Jesus and the Holy Spirit better, and to read your Bible every day. Our Lord and Savior Jesus Christ said in **John 14:15-18** and **16:5-15** that He would not leave us alone and that He will send us another helper, (**the Holy Spirit**), who would be in us and would guide us into all truth. And Jesus said in **John 14:18** that He will not leave us as orphans; **I will come to you**. So please believe in God and His Holy Word the Bible and remember to **Pray to the Holy Spirit** for help whenever you are being tempted to sin, because we really cannot live for God without His Help. If you want to become a Christian there is a Prayer for Salvation in the back of this book that you can pray to God and ask Him to save you, because everything written in this book applies to Christians, (Born Again Christians), and if you are not a Christian then none of what you have read will work for you.   The promises God has written in the Bible are for His children, (Born Again Believers), not un-believers.   And my prayer for you is that the Grace of the Lord Jesus Christ, and the Love of God, and the Communion of the Holy Spirit be with you always Amen! (**2 Corinthians 13:14**).   And remember to only believe God and the Bible, not men/women, and Check Everything Out before you Believe it, Amen.

CHAPTER 10

Tithes and Offerings

As a Born Again Believer in God and Jesus Christ you are supposed to Tithe to the Church, and then give Offerings if you can afford too.   Tithing was Commanded by God over 400 years before the law was given to Moses, Abraham tithe to God and he also gave a tithe to the King of Salem, (Melchizedek), in the Book of Genesis (**Genesis 14:18-20, Hebrews 7:1**).   Jacob, Isaac's son promises God that he will give back to Him a tenth of everything that God blesses him with (**Genesis 28:20-22**), this is a tithe and who do you think taught him this? Isaac his father of course, who learned it from Abraham his father.   As you can see from the very beginning God instituted away for His Children to be blessed financially, and that way is through the giving of tithes and offerings.   The Principles of how to tithe was explained in **Deuteronomy 14:22-27**, and the reasons why we tithe (**1**) is to Honor God with our possessions **Proverbs 3:9-10**, and (**2**) that we may learn to fear the Lord our God Always **Deuteronomy 14:23**.   You are going to run into some believers who are going to say that the tithe was food and not money, and they are correct in most cases, so if they want to tithe food then they should tithe food, but they must tithe something.   Most Churches have food pantries and clothes closets where people in need can come and get free food and clothing, they can give their food tithe to this ministry, and if your Church does not have one, then you can start one.   As you read the Old Testament in the Bible you can see time and time again how God blessed the people who believed in Him when they gave a tithe of what He gave them, and because of the blessings granted to them by God, some of them became very rich.   The same rules apply to Born Again Believers today, God gives us everything we need to live a comfortable life down here on earth if we use it wisely and don't spend more than we have, and we must also tithe 10 percent of our income to be financially blessed by God.   Tithing is a test of the heart for Born Again Believers, if you really trust God with all that you have then you will tithe, if you don't you won't, it's just that simple.   Jesus tells us in

(Matthew 6:21 and Luke 12:34), For where your treasure is, there will your heart be also.   If you can trust God and Jesus for your salvation from Hell, then you should also be able to trust Them with your money, because everything belongs to God anyway including you.   Through tithes and offerings, God allows Born Again Believers to assist Him in the spread of the Gospel of Jesus Christ while they are living down here on earth.   God does not need our money to complete His Salvation Plan, He is just allowing those who want to help out participate through the giving of tithes and offerings and other types of services.   Christians who really believe and trust God tithe their income and they volunteer their time and services in different ministries inside and outside of the Church if they can.   Their participation proves that they really Believe God and what He has written in the Bible and that they also trust Him with everything that they have including their money.   True Believers want to be a part of what God and Jesus are doing so they participate where they can just as James said in **James 2:14-22** faith without works is dead, and this is also the difference between **a Doer** of the Word and **a Hearer** of the Word (**James 1:22-25**).   For example, if your earthly mother or father asked you to do something for them would you do it, then why will you not do what God, (your Heavenly Father), asks you to do?   As Jesus taught us in the Parable of the Talents in (**Matthew 25:14-30**) when you follow God's instructions concerning money, He will bless you with more in the end, why, because you were faithful with a little, so now He can trust you with much more (**Luke 16:10**).   Just like in the Parable of the Talents God gives all of us our Talents/Salary to live off of while we are down here on earth (**Matthew 25:14-15**), and just as the owner of the business told his servants to do business until his return, God tells us the same, (the Great Commission to take the Gospel of Jesus Christ to the ends of the Earth).   In the Parable of the Talents, the owner does not tell his servants how to spend the money he gave them, just to do business until he returns, but God has told us how to spend 10 percent of the money He will give to us, we are to tithe 10 percent to His Church for the promotion of The Gospel of Jesus Christ His Son, and to make sure that there is food in His house (**Malachi 3:10-12**), and the rest you can spend as you will.   But please remember that in the Parable of the Talents the owner returned, and his servants had to give an account of what they did with the money he gave them, and we will do the same when we stand before Christ at His Judgement Seat, we will give an account for what we did or did not do with the money and other blessings He gave us while we were down here on Earth (**Romans 14:10 and 2Corinthians 5:10**).

God tells us in (**Malachi 3:10-12**); to bring all of the tithes into the storehouse, that there may be food in my house, **And Try Me Now In This Says The Lord of Hosts,** if I will not **open for you the windows of Heaven And pour out for you such a blessing** That there will not be room enough to receive it, Says The Lord of Hosts.

If you would take some time and study these scriptures you will see that God is telling us that if we tithe as we should, He will then bless us from Heaven, **this is a Promise from God,** and then on top of that He tells us to, (**AND TRY ME NOW IN THIS**), this is a test from God.   God is Daring Us to Tithe so that we will see Him bless us, and then we will know that He is telling us the Truth.   In the First Command from God He instructs us to bring our tithes into the storehouse, **and then He will open a window in Heaven** and bless you with more than you can handle, and after that He said **Now Put Me to The Test,** (**And Try Me Now in This**).   This is a **Double Dare** from Almighty God Himself to all Born Again Believers to let them know that He means what He Has Said in these scriptures and that He will take care of them if they do what He tells them to do, **Now Try Me In This** and put Me to the test says the **Lord of Host.**   This is a win-win situation for the Born Again Believer, you cannot lose, unless you do not do what God tells you to do (meaning; you do not tithe).   God has set it up so that we can only win because He said, (**AND TRY ME NOW IN THIS**), meaning to put Him to the test.   There is nothing else that I can tell you if Almighty God Himself said to **Put Me To The Test** and see won't I bless you, and you still do not tithe, then I don't know what else to say to you.   If you don't believe Him, I know you are not going to believe me, but I am going to tell you my testimony anyway and I hope it helps you to believe what God has said in these scriptures.   By the way, after I read **Malachi 3:10**, I did put God to the test as He said I could and He has never let me

139

down from that Sunday in April of 1999 until now.

Let's start with that Sunday, (the 2nd Sunday), in April of 1999 I
don't know the date, I could probably look it up but that's not important,
the lesson God taught me that day is what matters.   If you are like me
and listen to Christian Radio you know you hear all kinds of teachings
about tithes and offerings, some say to tithe, some say you don't have to
tithe and some say just give from your heart, all different and all sound
good to a point.   But this Sunday I was getting ready to go to church
and I was unsure of what to do, so as I was taking my shower, I begin to
Pray to God and I asked Him to teach me what I need to know about
tithes and offerings.   I said Father I need to know what to do and how
much to tithe, at that time I was giving 10 percent of my take home pay
check not the gross amount of my pay, and every time I would write the
check I felt funny inside, (I now know that this was the Holy Spirit
trying to tell me that I was giving the wrong amount, but back then I just
did not know this was Him trying to help me), so I asked God why do I
feel like I am not giving the right amount.   And then I said to God that I
cannot give 10 percent of the Gross Amount because I don't get the
gross amount of my pay before I get my paycheck the IRS takes out
taxes, and then God spoke to me through the Holy Spirit and said,
**(THAT IS CEASAR, NOW GIVE GOD WHAT BELONGS TO
GOD; Matthew 22:21, Mark 12:17 and Luke 20:25)**, I ACTUALLY
HEARD HIS VOICE.   And I just stood there in the shower stunned for
seem like minutes, so I said to myself I know I just heard a voice, and I
know that I am home alone and I know I am not crazy, so I then said
oooookkaaay.   So, I said okay Lord I now know that I must tithe, (but
How much), and then God sent to my mind all of the different scriptures
concerning the 10 percent tithe.   So, I got out of the shower knowing
exactly how much to tithe and why, so I went to church that Sunday and
tithe 10 percent of my gross paycheck (before taxes were taken out), and
I did not feel funny inside I had a peaceful feeling all over me, so I knew
what I had just done was right.   I was not looking for anything from
God, I was just doing what He had told me to do, and He had done
something for me that Sunday that money cannot buy, He spoke to me
and allowed me to hear His voice, so I know that God is real and no one

can tell me anything different. I don't hope, guest or think that He might be real, I know He is real. God met me where I was and He gave me the answer to my questions so that I could serve Him correctly, without any more doubt or confusion on my part. So on Monday, (the next day), when I went to work I got a raise in my pay, so the next Sunday came and I tithe 10 percent again, and the next day, (Monday), I got another raise in my pay, and then the 3rd Sunday in a row came and I tithed 10 percent again and on the next day, that Monday I got another raise in pay, 3 raises in pay in a row, now you know that was no one but God because there is no way that I was supposed to get 3 raises in a row on a job that I had only been working on for less than a year. And then on top of that to confirm His word to me about tithing, all of the 6 or 7 pastors that I listen to on Christian Radio were all doing a detail teaching on tithing, (the week after I gave my first tithe), so I knew what I had heard was true and what I was doing was Right, and from God. Now it is your turn, I can't promise you that you will get 3 raises in a row like I did but you never know because God is Good, if He did it for me, He might just do it for you. So, start tithing now, (**10 percent of your gross pay**), and just see how God blesses you for believing Him. Do not forget what I am about to say, (memorize this so you will not forget it), DO NOT TELL YOUR CO-WORKERS WHEN GOD GIVES YOU RAISES ON THE JOB, when they do not get one, they will all get mad at you when they find out. In my situation I did not tell my co-workers about the raises I received, I knew better from past experience, but someone from payroll did tell and all of my co-workers were mad at me. They were mad because I had only been on the job for less than a year, and now I was making more money than some of them were, because most of them had been working there for 8 years or more, man it was crazy LOL (Laugh out Loud), so don't do it. And be careful, because when God begins to bless you, you are going to now have a lot more extra money than you had before you did not tithe, and this can lead you into debt from overspending, and into all kinds of temptations that you have never experienced before, (Because you did not have the money before to do it), but now you will have a lot more available money and this can lead to trouble for some people (**1Timothy 6:8-10**). And don't go spending crazy either, remember to try and save some for a rainy day, and be very careful, don't let **Mark 4:19** come true in your life.   God does not promise to make all of us rich, if that was true then all Born Again Believers would be rich, (meaning money), because we are His children, and I think **Mark 4:19** and **1 Timothy 6:8-10** is the reason why He does not allow all of us to be materially rich, the money would draw us away from Him, and secondly God has commissioned us to take the Gospel of Jesus Christ to the poor, so this means that most of us will not be rich, how can you witness to the poor if you are rich.   The best witnesses are people who have been there and have done that, they have walked in the other person's shoes, so they can relate to them and their problems and understand exactly where they are coming from, and remember we are down here to do God's work not to get rich.   And also remember that God Loves a Cheerful Giver (**2Corinthians 9:6-7**). People always say this, but they never tell you why or that God is the One who makes you a Cheerful Giver.   Most people do not read **2Corinthians 9:8-11** where God tells you why you will be a Cheerful Giver, because He is taking care of you as He promised in **Malachi 3:10**, remember the Double Dare?

2Corinthians 9:8; And God is Able to Make **All Grace** abound Towards You, that You, **Always Having All Sufficiency in All Things**, **May Have Abundance** for Every Good Work.   (**9**) As it is written: "He has dispersed abroad, He has given to the poor; His righteousness endures forever." (**10**) Now may He who supplies seed to the sower, and bread for food, **supply and multiply the seed you have sown** and **increase the fruits of your righteousness**, (**11**) while **you are enriched in everything for all liberality**, which causes thanksgiving through us to God. (**12**) **For the administration of this service** not only supplies the needs of the saints, but also is abounding through many thanksgivings to God,

As you can see in **2Corinthians 9:8-12** if we begin to tithe as God commands us to, then He will bless us as He Promised in **Malachi 3:10**. Well, I hope this message will give you the faith that you need to trust God with all of your life including your finances.   Like God said in **Malachi 3:10" PUT ME TO THE TEST"**, the next step is now up to you, I have told you everything you need to know about tithing, now do it and see how God blesses you. Look up these scriptures and study them for yourself, don't just take my word for it, take them before God and ask Him to help you understand what they are teaching so you can do His will concerning the tithing of your finances. Offerings on the other hand are different, you give an offering if you can afford it. If you look up the offerings in the Old Testament you will see that all of them were for sins or trespasses except for 3, and in those 3 Offerings God asked the people to give, (only if they wanted to), for the building of the tabernacle, the temple and the objects that would go inside of them. Jesus Christ became our sin and trespass offering on the Cross at Calvary so we do not need to give offerings for sin, but there are some good offerings that you should give to if you can afford to, like (missions, the homeless, single mothers, food pantry at Church, Children's Church.... etc.), just check with your Church or look on the Church's bulletins they normally have them listed. Please remember that everything I have written about tithing is for Born Again Believers, God does not promise to bless the money given by un-believers, un-believers are not His Children. So, if you have been tithing and see no blessings in your life from God, then you need to ask yourself why, and then ask yourself if you have really given your life to Jesus Christ, meaning, have you asked Jesus Christ to be your Lord and Savior or has **James 4:3** come true in your life, and you just want the money to spend on yourself? **James 4:3** teaches us that if we are asking for money and things just to spend on ourselves or to show them off to others to brag about what we have and not used them to Glorify God, then He is not going to give it to us. And sadly, this kind of Greed has become the norm in the Church of Jesus Christ today. Believers are always asking God for all kinds of blessings, (financial as well as material), so that they can show them off or brag about what they have to their family, friends and to whoever will listen. This is not why God blesses us with money and things, He gives them to us to use to help others who are in need of help, and at the same time we ourselves are blessed by them too. Most Born Again Believers are not blessed financially because they do not tithe 10 percent of their income as God commanded them to in the Old Testament. They don't tithe or give offerings, but they have the nerve to ask God to bless them with money and things from His Kingdom, but they are not willing to put anything into His kingdom, meaning Tithes and Offerings, now does that sound fair to you?   Just because you are a Born Again child of God does not mean that He will automatically bless you financially, God promises to give us the things we need not the stuff we want or to make us rich (**Matthew 6:31-33**).   And furthermore, if you read the New Testament Bible you will not be able to find one person that God made rich simply because they became a Born Again Christian, Nowhere in the Bible **Not One person.**   Now go and Look in the New Testament Bible for yourself, and you will see that there is not one example of a person who gave their life to Jesus Christ and became a Born Again Christian, and then God made them rich, **No Not One**!

If you now understand that you should have been tithing all along, then start now, (next Sunday), go to God and ask Him to forgive you for not tithing in the past and then tell Him that you are starting now. Don't worry, God will forgive you because He knew you did not understand in the past, but now you do, and because He loves you and He wants the best for you, He will now give you another chance to believe and trust Him and the Bible.   So, stop chasing after money and the things of this world and turn your whole life and finances over to God, because everything belongs to Him anyway including you (**Psalm 24:1-2**).   Give the 10 percent tithe as God Commands us to and see how He blesses your entire life not just your finances.   We are the children of Almighty God and we are wealthier than we know, (even while we are living down here on earth), everything you see down here is ours through Jesus Christ our Lord, (Every House, Car, Building, Airplane…etc.), everything you see belongs to us, (Born Again Believers).   God has already given it to us in Jesus Christ through salvation (**1Corinthians 3:21-23**).   And God will only give some of it to those who **Believe and Trust** in Him, and to those that He can trust with it.   I know what you are going to say, but I know of a lot of people that are rich and do not believe in God, and that is true, but we don't know how they became rich either, or who they had to cheat/deceive or still from to get rich.   So just do it God's way and let Him bless you His way because God's way is always the best way to do anything.   And this is why God had all of the

Old Testament examples of tithing written down in the Bible so that we can learn from them, and at the same time we can see how God fulfilled his Promise and blessed the people who tithed (**Romans 15:4**).   And as I stated earlier God does not promise to make everyone rich who tithes, I am sure that there were a lot of believers not mentioned in the Bible who also tithed as they should and God did not make them rich, (yours truly included), but He did take care of them as He promised, and He will do the same for us.   If you want to become a Christian there is a Prayer for Salvation in the back of this book that you can Pray to God and ask Him to save you and to make you a Christian.   Believe Only the Word of God, not men/women, and Check Everything Out before you Believe it. Amen!

CHAPTER 11

TO THE CHURCH OF JESUS CHRIST
GOD STILL HEALS THE SICK

(**James 5:14-15**) (**14**) Is anyone among you sick?   Let him/her call for the Elders of the Church, and let them pray over him/her, anointing him/her with oil in the name of the Lord.

(**15**) And the prayer of faith will save the sick, and the Lord will raise him/her up.   And if he/she has committed sins, he/she will be forgiven.

If you are sick or you know of someone that is sick and need to be healed, then bring them to the Church and let **the Pastor and Elders** of the Church anoint them with oil and Pray over them in Jesus's name (**James 5:14-15**).   If they cannot come to the Church, then inform the Pastor and Elders and let them come to the person.   There are some **Born Again Believers** with the gift of healing because the Bible says so in (**1Corinthians 12:28-30**), so if you know of one then go to them for help, if not, then the Church of Jesus Christ is where we should bring people who are sick to be healed by God.   And make sure you ask the Pastor and the Elders that will Pray over you if they are **Born Again/Saved,** if they are not Born Again then do not let them Pray over you, it will do you no Good because **God uses Born Again Believers** to heal people, not un-believers.   If He allows un-believers to heal people then the scripture above is of no effect (**James 5:14-15**), and we would have false healers all over the place and no one will give God the praise and glory for the healing, they will give it to the person that healed them, like the false healers you see on T.V.   This scripture teaches us that **God uses Born Again Believers to Heal the Sick**, the person who is sick does not have to be a Christian/ Born Again to be healed, God will still heal the person because of the **Born Again Pastor and Elders** who are praying for that persons healing.   In this day and time, (that we live in), there are so many false teachers/un-saved men and women out there in the world that are calling themselves preachers of Almighty God that we must now ask Them if they are saved to be sure, and don't be afraid to ask them because the Bible teaches us in **2 Corinthians 11:13-15** that satan's ministers will try to pass themselves off as ministers of God. And the most important reason why you must ask is because you want to be healed by God of your illness, and God only heals people by His methods, not by the methods of men/women and the world. God Heals believers and un-believers this way so that people inside and outside of the Church will know that He is Real, and that He Still Heals people of their sicknesses, just as Jesus did in the Bible when people came to Him for help.

You always hear a pastor, or someone say that Jesus did not Heal Everybody, **(that is a Lie)**, everywhere in the Bible when you see Jesus Healing people the scriptures always say, and **He Healed Everybody brought to Him (Matthew 4:23-24, 8:16-17, 9:35, 12:15, 14:14, 14:34-36 and 15:30-31)**. So, bring all of your sick family and friends to Church so God can heal them if this is His Will. **God will get the Glory** for the healing, and the Healings will edify the Church of Jesus Christ and its members by strengthening their Faith in God and the Bible **(Matthew 9:1-8)**. The members of the Church will see with their own eyes that God still heals, and these healings will be the proof that some of them will need to complete their faith in God, where after seeing this **Healing Miracle** they will now turn their whole life over to Him. And you never know, the person who was healed might even Give their life to Jesus Christ. In the Gospels, Jesus Christ healed people of every type of disease, illness, physical defect and demon possession, so whatever your family, friends or associates are suffering from do not hesitate to tell them that God can heal them and help them get better.

Steps to Getting Healed

The first thing to remember is that all healings are done by God for the Glory of God. The man or woman that He uses to pray over you is not the healer, God is the healer so do not give the person the glory that belongs to God. And do not go to these fake healers you see on T.V., these people are just using the name of God and Christ to make money, and most of the people there that really need to be healed are never healed, the camera never shines on them or the people in wheelchairs. And most important of all you never see these so called T.V. healers at Hospitals Healing Children or people that are really sick. When I see one of them at a Children's Hospital healing sick children, then I will believe that he/she is a healer sent by God.

Now let's get to the Steps that you should take to ask God to heal you. Before you ask God to heal you, the most important step in the process is the way that you approach God to ask Him to heal you. A lot of you watch too much T.V. or you are listening to people/Christians who are giving you false information about how to get God to do what you want Him to do, and you come to God demanding that He heals you or do this or that for you, (Really!!). First of all, do not forget who you are talking to, **He is the Almighty God of Heaven and Earth**, **God is Holy** and you do not approach Him in any kind of way, you humble yourself when you come to Him because **He is God**. You are lucky that God does not give you what you really deserve, (A Lightning Bolt), for coming to Him in an un-worthy manner, but because He loves us and He knows everything, He overlooks our ignorance and He does not punish us for our wrong approach towards Him. You do not demand anything from God, you ask Him for what you need, and then He might give it to you, and if He does not, then you do not need It, it is just that simple. So you don't have to keep praying for it over and over again, when God wants you to have something, He will give it to you. Now sometimes He tells us to wait, and when this happens, He will place a peaceful feeling inside of you letting you know that what you have asked for you will get, just not right now, He never leaves us just hanging and hoping. If you do not have a peaceful feeling inside of you that you will get your request in the future, then God's answer is NO, so stop asking for that particular thing or person over and over again. You must come to God in humility when you want something from Him, and especially if you want to be healed. In almost every case in the Bible where I see Jesus healing an individual, the person needing to be healed always came to Him saying "**Lord Jesus Son of David Have Mercy on Me...**", not demanding or naming and claiming something, but "**LORD**

JESUS Have Mercy on Me…" and then Jesus will ask them what do you need, and then He would heal them (**Matthew 9:27-31, 15:21-28, 17:14-18 and 20:29-34**).   In the Bible, these people never came to Jesus demanding anything because they knew that they needed his help, and they also knew that no one else could help them but Him.   Some of us are not healed because of the way we approached God when we asked for our healing.   Use the Bible as your example and pray to God and say **Father God please Have Mercy on Me**…, and then ask for your healing in Jesus's name, and God may heal you, now let's go to step 1.

STEP 1: You yourself pray to God and ask Him to heal you.

If you are a Born Again Christian, then you are a child of God and you can ask Him for whatever you need, and He might give it to you if it is His will.   But you must be **Born Again/Saved**, un-believers cannot get anything from God until they become Born Again children of God, a Born Again Believer can pray for them and God might grant their request, but only because the Born Again person has prayed for them, this is called intercessory prayer.   God is our Father and He loves us, so when we are sick and hurting our first response should be to go to Him for healing and comfort, because He really cares and loves us as He tells us in (**1Peter 5:6-7**).   So, go to God first by yourself, and ask Him to heal you of your sickness, and if He heals you, then you will know for yourself that God still heals, and then you will glorify God and thank Him for this **Healing Miracle.**   This healing miracle will make your faith in Him more stronger than ever, and you will be a living witness of God's instant healing power in today's world.   You will be a living witness to your family, friends and others to let them know that God still heals just like He did in the Bible.

Step 1 does work, (I am a living witness of this myself), I am a truck driver and I had a job where I delivered new trucks from the factory to the truck dealerships or to the customer.   Have you ever been driving down the road and you saw some trucks going down the road standing up leaning on one another, if so then you might have seen me, this is how we deliver new trucks to dealerships or customers? All of those trucks could be going to the same dealer or to separate dealers somewhere in the US, Canada or overseas. One year I had a trip to Canada to deliver 3 trucks and on the way up there I sprang my ankle somehow, to this day I do not know how I did it, but when I reached my hotel for the night I could barely walk. So, after checking into the hotel, I showered and laid down and put a bag of ice on my ankle trying to make the swelling go down while I slept. I know what to do because I have hurt my ankle many times, and I have been to emergency rooms for the injury, and they all gave me the same treatment information, take the pain pills, ice it and stay off of it for 3 days, so I knew the routine. But this time I was not at home I was in a hotel room in Edmonton Alberta Canada, where I knew no one and I did not know if the hospitals would treat me because I was not a citizen of Canada, and this was a bad sprang, I could barely walk. So, when I woke up the next morning there was no change in my ankles condition, so I began to Pray to God and I asked Him to **have mercy on me and to heal my ankle**. I told Him that I was far from home and He was the only one that I knew who could help me and heal me. I prayed to Him and told Him that He was my Father and that He made me, so I knew He could heal me, so at that time mother nature called and I had to go to the bathroom. Now my troubles really began, because with a bad ankle you cannot just jump up and walk to the bathroom, no you have to plan each step and pick a path of movement. There was a chair I could use for support, but it was about two steps away from me, so I knew I would have to take one step on my hurt ankle, (I knew this was going to hurt), but the bathroom was calling, so I took that one step and made it to the chair and I felt the sharp pain of my ankle hurting, so I now knew that it was a bad sprang and that I needed to go to the hospital. So, while standing in the bathroom I prayed to God again and said Father I know you can heal me so that I can complete my job here, so please heal me now Father, I need you Now, but if you don't heal me, then I know it is for a reason, so let your will be done. So, I turned to come out of the bathroom and I grabbed the chair for support and I took one step to the dresser and after making it I realized that the pain was not so bad, so I took another step and then another one without the chair, and then I was standing at my bed fully healed.   So, I thanked God my Father and I turned around and I walked to the room's front door and then back to my bed, and I thanked and Glorified God for healing me as I was walking back and forth in my room.   Later that morning I ate breakfast and made my delivery in Edmonton Alberta Canada, and I then drove the last truck to Vancouver B.C. Canada.   So, I know that God still heals, (**and instantly**), because He did it for me, I am a living witness.   Amen.

Step 2: Call 2 or 3 Born Again Believers together to pray with and over you for your healing.

(**Matthew 18:20**) For where 2 or 3 are gathered together in My name, **I am there in the mist of them**.

(**James 5:16**) Confess your trespasses to one another, **and Pray for one another, that you may be healed**.   The effective, fervent Prayer of a righteous man avails much.

In (**Matthew 18:20**) Jesus teaches us that when 2 or 3 of us come together in His name that He is in the mist of us.   So, while we are together helping and praying for others, we also should pray for one another if we are sick and need to be healed.   And if God heals the person that we prayed for, then we will all glorify God together and we all will be living witnesses of God's instant healing power toward that person.   God will get the glory and the Praying Born Again Believers faith in God will be strengthen, because they will have experienced for themselves the Healing Power of God.   This Healing Miracle is something that they would have seen and experienced for themselves, and not something they heard someone else say or something they read in a book.   No, they would have experienced and saw this with their own eyes, and no one would be able to tell them that God does not heal anymore because they will know for themselves that He can, and this healing will be something that they will remember for the rest of their lives.   Now, after 2 or 3 Born Again Believers have prayed for you and God did not heal you, then you must go to step 3.

Step 3: Go to the Elders of the Church.

In (**James 5:14-15**), the Bible teaches us to go to the Elders of the Church to be healed by God. Out of the 3 ways given for being healed by God, this is the main way because God wants mankind to know that He is real and that He Still heals, and that they still must come to Him when they need to be healed, plus the healing Miracles Will Glorify GOD and the Church of His Son Jesus Christ and strengthen the faith and witness of the followers of Christ. To be healed by God you must do it His way and follow the steps that He has outlined for us to follow inside of the Bible, God is only going to honor the things that He has told us to believe and do, He is not going to honor something made up by men/women that cannot be found in the Bible. So, false teachings like positive professing and naming and claiming will not get you healed by God, because they cannot be found inside of His Holy Word the Bible. We must do it His way, and God has already told us how to be healed by Him in **James 5:14-15**, Step **1**. Call or go to the Elders of the Church, (make sure that **the Elders are Born Again/Saved** are you might not be healed), Step **2**. Let them Pray over you, anointing you with oil in the name of the Lord, and if it's His will to heal you then He will heal you. Doctors cannot really heal you, they can only tell you what they think is wrong with you, God does all of the healing of believers as well as un-believers through the Holy Spirit of God who lives inside of all Born Again/Saved Christians. Why does he heal un-believers? Because there are Born Again believers somewhere praying for them, someone who knows that they are sick has asked a believer to pray for them, and then God answers that Born Again/Saved Christians prayer request. Healings done in the house of God will make some people who probably would have never step foot in a Church recognize that if they want to be healed then they must come to God, in His house and on His terms. Because there are millions of people who do not believe that God is real, and millions more who know that He is probably real but refuse to believe and honor Him. So, God has placed healing inside the Church of His Son, (Jesus Christ), to draw those who want to be healed to Him and to let everyone know that Jesus Christ is the Only way to God and His healings and not all of these other false religions who do not Honor

His Son.   We as believers need to get the message out to our family and friends that if they want to be healed of whatever is bothering them, then they need to come to the House of God, the Church of Jesus Christ to ask God to heal them.

All of the Churches of Jesus Christ should send out Prayer teams of Pastors and Elders to every children's hospital to heal the Children of their diseases.   Some Church's do have prayer teams, but not all Churches do this, it all boils down to if you believe what is written in the Bible or not.   The Church's that believe in God and His Holy Word the Bible, they have Prayer Teams and they send them out to pray for people, the Churches who do not believe God and the Bible don't.   I hope and pray that believers will believe in God and the Bible and start being Doers of the Word and not just Hearers of His Word because there are a lot of sick people in the world that are dying and all they had to do was to come to God for the help that they needed (**James 1:22-25**).   It is time for Born Again Believers to begin to lead people back to the House of God, (the Church of Jesus Christ), for the healings and the spiritual help that they need, and you can start with your own family and friends, just let them know that God still heals, and you never know they might say yes.

Finally, if you have tried steps 1-3 and God still did not heal you, then you must now go to God in prayer and ask Him why?   Ask God what is going on in your life that is preventing Him from healing you. This health problem could be a trial caused by, disobedience, punishment for sin, unhealthy living, by taking the Lord's supper in an un-worthy manner, or it's just time for the person to die.   But in most cases, things like this happens to believers when they neglect God and try to live their lives without Him or they are not doing what He has told them to do. Whatever the case is you now must stop what you are doing and go to God for your answer, (Right Now), He is the only one who can tell you what is going on and why He has not healed you.   This happened to me before I started to write this book.   I was so busy at work that I was not setting aside any time to write the book God was telling me to write, so in January of 2011, God told me through the Holy Spirit that I needed to start writing.   I was working one day and a thought came to my mind saying you need to be writing.   I knew it was from God because I was thinking about something totally different, and I said yes Lord.   As the year went along, every month I would hear this voice saying the same message, (**You need to be writing**), but I was so busy at work I continued to forget to stop and set aside some time to write.   So, on October 19, 2011, God allowed me to get hurt at work, and as soon as I realized that I was hurt bad I knew why because I was not writing as God had told me too.   So, 2 days later I went to the emergency room because the pain would not stop, and after the doctors checked me out, they told me that I would be off of work for a while because I had torn my rotator cuff in my shoulder.   It felt like 10,000 pounds of pressure was lifted off of my shoulders when I heard the message that I would be off of work for a while because I knew that I should have been writing and now I could do what God wanted me to do and not worry about going to work at a job.   So as soon as I got home from the emergency room I sat down at the computer and started to write, this was about 10 am in the morning, the next time I look up it was night, I could not believe it, I had been writing all day and for most of the night.   I was not tired or hungry for food, I had been so focused on God and writing that I lost all track of time and space, I heard no noises or sounds, I was totally drawn into God and the Bible.   And this is how this book came about, but God had to allow me to be hurt to get me to do what He knew I needed to be doing, which was His will and not mine, and that was for me to writing this book at that time and not later.   So, you must now go to God in prayer and ask Him why you have not been healed if you do not have any idea, and He will let you know why.   You might not like God's answer because it will be a part of His will and plans for your life and not yours. If you don't like His answer don't get mad and become stubborn, my advice to you is to do what God is telling you to do because the illness is not going anywhere until you do.   May God bless you, Amen.

PRAYER FOR SALVATION

Dear God,

Please help me I am a sinner.

I know I am living wrong and I need you to help me by saving me from my sins.

I believe that Jesus Christ is your Son and that He died on the Cross for the Forgiveness of all of my Sins past, present and future.

I also believe in my heart that you raised Him from the dead.

Jesus, I now ask you to come into my life and become my Lord and savior and save me from my sins.

Father God please fill me with your Holy Spirit so that He can change me into the person that you want me to be.

Thank you, God for saving me, now please help me to follow and serve you for the rest of my life

In Jesus name I pray.   Amen!

PRAYING IN THE SPIRIT

If You want The Holy Spirit of God to lead Your Prayers,
Then Pray This Prayer to God Before You Start to Pray.

Dear Heavenly Father,

I Surrender My Mind, My Soul and My Spirit to You Right Now Father for Your Direction. Father God can you Please Fill Me with Your Holy Spirit Right Now, so that He Can Guide Me in My Prayers. Holy Spirit please direct me as I Pray so that I Will Know What to Pray, and Who to Pray For according to God's will. Thank You Father for Helping Me to Pray.

In Jesus Name I Pray, Amen.

BIBLE ANSWERS TO SOME IMPORTANT QUESTIONS

How to Say NO to Sin God's Way

DAILY THINGS TO DO FOR VICTORY OVER YOUR SIN

1. You must Pray to God and ask Him for Help with your sin problem. So, every morning before I get out of bed I Pray this Prayer to God.
Father God, I know I am going to be tempted today (name areas you are normally tempted in daily), so please fill me with your Holy Spirit so when these temptations come my way today, the Holy Spirit will give me the power to say no to them. Because if you do not help me Father I know I am going to fall into sin, and I do not want to sin against you, the Lord Jesus or the Holy Spirit.   So please help me, in Jesus name I pray Amen.

2. You must present your body and mind to Him every day as living sacrifices and ask Him to keep them from sin. **Romans 12:1-2, 6:12-14, 16, 19**

3. You must identify the people, places or things that tempt you to sin, and then to the best of your ability you must stay away from them until God has given you the strength to say no to them when you are tempted by them.

4. Remember that Jesus delivered us from the Power of sin through salvation, being Born Again. **Romans 8:3-5, 7:24-25**

5. God will give life to our mortal bodies through the Holy Spirit so we can say no to our sins when we are tempted. **Romans 8:9-13**

6. God Promises that the Holy Spirit will be there to help us in our weaknesses. **Romans 8:26**

7. God Promises believers in **Romans 8:31** that we do not have to

worry about anyone or anything because if He is for us then who can be against us. Because He is **The ALL POWERFUL GOD** of Heaven and Earth.

8. You must believe God, you must be **fully convinced** that Everything that God has spoken in the Bible is True, and whatever He has promised He is able to perform. **Romans 4:20-25**

SOME OF THE GREAT AND AWESOME PROMISES FROM GOD TO HIS CHILDREN, "BORN AGAIN CHRISTIANS".

1John 4:4; God Promises Born Again Believers that He Who is Inside of You, (The Holy Spirit), is Greater Than he who is in the World, (satan and demons).

1Corinthians 10:13; God will only allow us to be tempted with what we can bear.

James 1:5; God will give us wisdom if we ask Him for it.

Matthew 11:28-30; Jesus promises His followers rest from the things of the world if they follow Him.

Philippians 4:4-7; God will give us the peace that surpasses all understanding.

Psalm 92:12-15; We can continue to be strong and bear fruit to God as we age.

Psalm 46:1-3, Hebrews 13:5-6; God will help us in times of trouble, therefore we should not fear.

Psalm 32:8; God said that He will instruct and teach us the way we should go.   And I will guide you with My EYE, says the Lord.

Psalm 103:1-4; God will heal us in times of sickness.

Romans 8:38-39; Nothing can separate us from the Love of God.

John 10:27-30, Hebrews 7:25, 1John 5:9-13; God and Jesus Promises **Eternal Security** to Born Again Christians.

John 14:1-3; Jesus Promises believers that we will be in Heaven with Him.

Psalm 32:10; He who trusts in the Lord, mercy shall surround him/her.

Romans 8:14-17, Galatians 3:26-29, 4:7 and Ephesians 1:1-14 Born Again Christians are now children of God, and they now have a Proud Family Heritage to claim and apply to their life as their own.

1John 1:9; We have daily forgiveness for our sins so we can stay clean and close to God.

Hebrews 13:5; God Promises that He will Never Leave nor Fore Sake us, and that we should be content with what He has given us.

John 14:16-18, Romans 8:26; Jesus Promises Believers that God will give us the Holy Spirit who will teach, guide and help us in times of weakness.

Isaiah 41:9-13; God will strengthen and help us in times of trouble, fear not-don't panic.

Matthew 6:25, Philippians 4:19; God Promises to meet all of our needs, (not wants), if we seek first the Kingdom of God.

1John 5:14-15; God will Answer our Prayers if we Pray according to His Will.

Psalm 84:11; No Good thing does He uphold from those who walk uprightly.

2Corinthians 1:3-4; God Promises to comfort us in times of trouble so that we can comfort others in their times of trouble.

BIBLE SCRIPTURE
REFERENCE SECTION

The Book of Romans
Chapters 4, 5, 6, 7, 8

Romans 4

[19] And not being weak in faith, he considered not his own body now dead, when he was about a hundred years old, neither yet the deadness of Sarah's womb:

[20] He staggered not at the promise of God through unbelief; but was strong in faith, giving glory to God;

[21] And being **fully persuaded** that, **what he had promised, he was able also to perform**.

[22] And therefore it was imputed to him for righteousness.

[23] **Now it was not written for his sake alone**, that it was imputed to him;

[24] But for us also, **to whom it shall be imputed, if we believe on him** that raised up Jesus our Lord from the dead;

[25] **Who was delivered for our offences**, and was raised again for our justification

Romans 5

5 1Therefore being justified by faith, **we have peace with God through our Lord Jesus Christ**:

[2] By whom also **we have access by faith into this grace wherein we stand**, and rejoice in hope of the glory of God.

[3] And not only so, but we glory in tribulations also: knowing that tribulation produces patience;

[4] And patience, experience; and experience, hope:

[5] And hope does not disappoint, because the love of God is shed abroad in our hearts by **the Holy Ghost which is given unto us.**

[6] For when we were yet without strength, in due time Christ died for the ungodly.

[7] For scarcely for a righteous man will one die: yet peradventure for a good man some would even dare to die.

[8] But God **demonstrates his love toward us**, in that, **while we were yet sinners, Christ died for us.**

[9] Much more then, **being now justified by his blood, we shall be saved from wrath through him**.

[10] For if, when we were enemies, we were reconciled to God by the death of his Son, much more, being reconciled, we shall be saved by his life.

[11] And not only so, but we also joy in **God through our Lord Jesus Christ, by whom we have now received the atonement.**

[12] Wherefore, as **by one man sin entered into the world**, and death by sin; **and so death passed upon all men, for that all have sinned:**

[13] (For until the law sin was in the world: but sin is not imputed when there is no law.

[14] Nevertheless death reigned from Adam to Moses, even over them that had not sinned after the similitude of Adam's transgression, who is the figure of him that was to come.

¹⁵ But not as the offence, so also is the free gift. For if through the offence of one many be dead, much more the grace of God, and the gift by grace, which is by one man, Jesus Christ, hath abounded unto many.

¹⁶ And not as it was by one that sinned, so is the gift: for the judgment was by one to condemnation, but the free gift is of many offences unto justification.

¹⁷ For if by one man's offence death reigned by one; much more they which receive abundance of grace and of the gift of righteousness shall reign in life by one, Jesus Christ.)

¹⁸ Therefore as by the offence of one judgment came upon all men to condemnation; even so by the righteousness of one **the free gift** came upon all men unto justification of life.

¹⁹ For as **by one man's disobedience many were made sinners**, so **by the obedience of one shall many be made righteous.**

²⁰ Moreover the law entered, that the offence might abound. But where sin abounded, grace did much more abound:

²¹ That as sin hath reigned unto death, even so might grace reign through righteousness unto eternal life **by Jesus Christ our Lord.**

Romans 6

6 What shall we say then? Shall we continue in sin, that grace may abound?

² God forbid. **How shall we, that are dead to sin,** live any longer therein?

³ Know ye not, that so many of us as were baptized into Jesus Christ were baptized into his death?

⁴ Therefore we are buried with him by baptism into death: that like as Christ was raised up from the dead by the glory of the Father, even so **we also should walk in newness of life**.

⁵ For if we have been planted together in the likeness of his death, we shall be also in the likeness of his resurrection:

⁶ Knowing this, **that our old man is crucified with him, that the body of sin might be destroyed, that we should no longer be slaves of sin.**

⁷ For he that is dead is freed from sin.

⁸ Now if we be dead with Christ, we believe that we shall also live with him:

⁹ Knowing that Christ being raised from the dead dies no more; death hath no more dominion over him.

¹⁰ For in that he died, he died to sin once for all; but the life that he lives, he lives unto God.

¹¹ **Likewise you also, reckon yourselves to be dead indeed unto sin**, but alive unto God through Jesus Christ our Lord.

¹² **Let not sin therefore reign in your mortal body, that you should obey it in its lusts.**

¹³ **Neither yield your members as instruments of unrighteousness unto sin: but yield yourselves unto God, as those that are alive from the dead, and your members as instruments of righteousness unto God.**

[14] **For sin shall not have dominion over you**: for you are not under the law, but under grace.

[15] What then? Shall we sin, because we are not under the law, but under grace? God forbid.

[16] **Know you not, that to whom you yield yourselves servants to obey, his servants you are to whom you obey; whether of sin unto death, or of obedience unto righteousness?**

[17] But God be thanked, that you were the servants of sin, but you have obeyed from the heart that form of doctrine which was delivered you.

[18] **Being then made free from sin**, you became the servants of righteousness.

[19] I speak after the manner of men because of the weakness of your flesh: for as you have yielded your members servants to uncleanness and to lawlessness unto more lawlessness; **so now yield your members servants to righteousness unto holiness.**

[20] For when you were the slaves of sin, you were free from righteousness.

[21] What fruit had you then in **those things whereof you are now ashamed?** For the end of those things is death.

[22] **But now being made free from sin, and become servants to God, you have your fruit unto holiness, and the end everlasting life.**

[23] **For the wages of sin is death; but the gift of God is eternal life through Jesus Christ our Lord.**

Romans 7

7 Or do you not know, brethren, (for I speak to them that know the law,) how that the law has dominion over a man as long as he lives?

² For the woman who has a husband is bound by the law to her husband as long as he lives; but if the husband be dead, she is loosed from the law of her husband.

³ So then if, while her husband lives, she be married to another man, she shall be called an adulteress: but if her husband dies, she is free from that law; so that she is no adulteress, though she be married to another man.

⁴ Therefore, my brethren, **you also have become dead to the law through the body of Christ**; that you should be married to another, to him who is raised from the dead, that we should bear fruit unto God.

⁵ **For when we were in the flesh, the sinful passions** which were aroused by the law were **at work in our members to bear fruit unto death.**

⁶ **But now we have been delivered from the law,** having died to what we were held by, so **that we should serve in newness of the spirit**, and not in the oldness of the letter.

⁷ What shall we say then? Is the law sin? God forbid. On the contrary, I would not have known sin except through the law.   For I would not have known covetousness except the law had said, Thou shalt not covet.

⁸ But sin, taking occasion by the commandment, produced in me all manner of evil desire. For without the law sin was dead.

⁹ For I was alive without the law once: but when the commandment came, sin revived, and I died.

¹⁰ And the commandment, which was to bring life, I found to bring death.

¹¹ **For sin, taking occasion by the commandment, deceived me, and by it slew me.**

¹² Wherefore the law is holy, and the commandment holy, and just, and good.

¹³ Was then that which is good made death unto me? God forbid. **But sin, that it might appear sin**, working death in me by that which is good; **that sin by the commandment might become exceeding sinful.**

¹⁴ For we know that the law is spiritual: but I am carnal, sold under sin.

¹⁵ **For what I am doing, I do not understand. For what I will to do, that I do not practice; but what I hate, that I do.**

¹⁶ If, then, I do what I will not to do, I agree with the law that it is good.

¹⁷ Now then it is no longer I who do it, but sin that dwells in me.

¹⁸ **For I know that in me (that is, in my flesh,) nothing good dwells; for to will is present with me; but how to perform that which is good I find not.**

¹⁹ **For the good that I will to do, I do not do; but the evil I will not to do, that I do.**

²⁰ Now if I do what I will not to do, it is no more I that do it, **but sin that dwells in me.**

²¹ I find then a law, that, **when I would do good, evil is present with me**.

²² For I delight in the law of God after the inward man:

²³ But I see another law in my members, **warring against the law of my mind, and bringing me into captivity to the law of sin which is in my members.**

²⁴ O wretched man that I am! **Who will deliver me from this body of this death?**

²⁵ **I thank God through Jesus Christ our Lord**. So then, with the mind I myself serve the law of God; but with the flesh the law of sin.

Romans 8

8 There is therefore **now no condemnation to them which are in Christ Jesus, who walk not after the flesh, but after the Spirit.**

² **For the law of the Spirit of life in Christ Jesus hath made me free from the law of sin and death**.

³ For what the law could not do, in that it was weak through the flesh, **God sending his own Son in the likeness of sinful flesh, and for sin, condemned sin in the flesh:**

⁴ **That the righteousness of the law might be fulfilled in us, who walk not after the flesh, but after the Spirit.**

⁵ **For they that are after the flesh set their minds on the things of the flesh; but they that are after the Spirit the things of the Spirit.**

⁶ For to be carnally minded is death; **but to be spiritually minded is life and peace.**

⁷ **Because the carnal mind is enmity against God**: for it is not subject to the law of God, neither indeed can be.

⁸ So then they that are in the flesh cannot please God.

⁹ But you are not in the flesh, but in the Spirit, if indeed the Spirit of God dwells in you. Now if any man have not the Spirit of Christ, he is none of his.

¹⁰ And if Christ be in you, the body is dead because of sin; but the Spirit is life because of righteousness.

¹¹ But if the Spirit of him that raised up Jesus from the dead dwell in you, he that raised up Christ from the dead shall also quicken your mortal bodies by his Spirit that dwells in you.

¹² Therefore, brethren, we are debtors, not to the flesh, to live after the flesh.

¹³ For if you live after the flesh, you shall die: but if you through the Spirit put to death the deeds of the body, you shall live.

¹⁴ For as many as are led by the Spirit of God, they are the sons of God.

¹⁵ For you have not received the spirit of bondage again to fear; but you have received the Spirit of adoption, whereby we cry, Abba, Father.

¹⁶ The Spirit itself bears witness with our spirit, that we are the children of God:

¹⁷ And if children, then heirs; heirs of God, and joint-heirs with Christ; **if so be that we suffer with him, that we may be also glorified together.**

¹⁸ For I reckon that the sufferings of this present time are not worthy to be compared with the glory which shall be revealed in us.

¹⁹ For the earnest expectation of the creation waits for the manifestation of the sons of God.

²⁰ For the creation was made subject to vanity, not willingly, but by reason of him who hath subjected the same in hope,

²¹ Because the creature itself also shall be delivered from the bondage of corruption into the glorious liberty of the children of God.

²² For we know that the whole creation groans and labors in pain together until now.

²³ And not only they, but ourselves also, which have the firstfruits of the Spirit, even we ourselves groan within ourselves, waiting for the adoption, to wit, the redemption of our body.

²⁴ For we are saved by hope: but hope that is seen is not hope: for what a man sees, why doth he yet hope for?

²⁵ But if we hope for that we see not, then do we with patience wait for it.

²⁶ **Likewise the Spirit also helps in our weaknesses**: for we know not what we should pray for as we ought: but the Spirit itself makes intercession for us with groanings which cannot be uttered.

²⁷ And he that searches the hearts knows what the mind of the Spirit is, **because he makes intercession for the saints according to the will of God.**

²⁸ **And we know that all things work together for good to them that love God, to them who are the called according to his purpose.**

²⁹ For whom he did foreknow, **he also did predestinate to be conformed to the image of his Son, that he might be the firstborn among many brethren.**

[30] Moreover whom he did predestinate, them he also called: and whom he called, them he also justified: and whom he justified, them he also glorified.

[31] What shall we then say to these things? **If God be for us, who can be against us?**

[32] **He that spared not his own Son, but delivered him up for us all,** how shall he not with him also freely give us all things?

[33] Who shall lay anything to the charge of God's elect? It is God that justifies.

[34] Who is he that condemns? **It is Christ that died, yea rather, that is risen again, who is even at the right hand of God, who also makes intercession for us.**

[35] Who shall separate us from the love of Christ? Shall tribulation, or distress, or persecution, or famine, or nakedness, or peril, or sword?

[36] As it is written, "For Your sake we are killed all the day long; we are accounted as sheep for the slaughter.

[37] Yet in all these things we are more than conquerors through him that loved us.

[38] **For I am persuaded, that neither death, nor life, nor angels, nor principalities, nor powers, nor things present, nor things to come,**

[39] Nor height, nor depth, nor any other creature, **shall be able to separate us from the love of God, which is in Christ Jesus our Lord.**

About the Author

He is a Born Again Christian who was being defeated by sin and temptation until God taught him these truths written inside of this book.   His hearts desire is to get this information to all Christians so that they can start having victory over their sins and temptations also.   This is why God told him to write this book, Amen.

One More Thing

If you like this book, then go to **www.amazon.com** and write a honest review letting other people know what you think about the book.   Thank you for your support.

Made in the USA
Columbia, SC
14 March 2021

34272519R00105